VALUE-BASED LEADERSHIP IN PUBLIC PROFESSIONS

Value-based Leadership in Public Professions

Tor Busch

Professor Emeritus, Trondheim Business School, Norway

and

Alex Murdock

*Professor of Not for Profit Management and Leadership,
London South Bank University*

First published 2014 by
PALGRAVE MACMILLAN

Palgrave Macmillan in the UK is an imprint of Macmillan Publishers Limited, registered in England, company number 785998, of Houndmills, Basingstoke, Hampshire RG21 6XS.

Palgrave Macmillan in the US is a division of St Martin's Press LLC, 175 Fifth Avenue, New York, NY 10010.

Palgrave Macmillan is the global academic imprint of the above companies and has companies and representatives throughout the world.

Palgrave® and Macmillan® are registered trademarks in the United States, the United Kingdom, Europe and other countries.

ISBN 978–1–137–33109–0

This book is printed on paper suitable for recycling and made from fully managed and sustained forest sources. Logging, pulping and manufacturing processes are expected to conform to the environmental regulations of the country of origin.

A catalogue record for this book is available from the British Library.

A catalog record for this book is available from the Library of Congress.

Typeset by MPS Limited, Chennai, India.

Printed in China.

Contents

Discovery Library

Tel: 01752 439111

List of Figures

Preface

This book is directed at students studying public-sector management. It is also relevant for the professional practitioner and manager in the public setting. It seeks to offer a blend of grounded theoretical understanding beyond that found in purely practitioner publications of the "How to Succeed in Management" variety. However, it is also consciously written in an accessible and readable style to enable it to be accessed by a general readership. Both authors have many years of experience as professionals, managers, academic researchers, and teachers. The authors also intend the book to have an application across national boundaries.

The concept of leadership has been the subject of academic debate and exploration for almost as long as history has been recorded. It has been explicit in the military setting and has also been the subject of a wide range of literature in the business arena.

Similarly, public administration has had a long and distinguished academic tradition reaching back to antiquity. Much of the history of public administration has significant links with religion, especially in Europe. This shows the connections between some concept of values and public administration. Indeed, values are implicit in many of the reforms which have occurred in the development of public administration. The Weberian bureaucracy carried with it a strong presumption of values of neutrality and adherence to process as contrasted to the values associated with nepotism which preceded it.

In the last 30 years, public administration has been heavily influenced by what has been described as "New Public Management," which valued effectiveness and efficiency often with a preference for techniques imported from the business or private sector. Public administrators became translated into public managers with a presumption of a different division of responsibility between manager and the politician. There are parallels between the relationship between the board and the managers in a company. However, whilst the private manager has a focus upon enhancing shareholder value, the public manager is tasked with public value.

The age of New Public Management has become tempered by a perception of an increasing requirement for public governance, reflecting a view that public bodies need to be regulated in ways which are not simply a matter of managerial diktat. The roles of the public manager and the elected politician, clearly distinguished under the public administration and New Public Management traditions, may become subject to a new development with an emerging research literature on new public leadership.

This concept of value-based leadership which is the focus of this book is in the tradition of these developments. Value-based leadership, as the book will explore, has particular relevance for the public sector and for managers in the public sector. The civil service detachment espoused in traditional public administration carried with it a strong sense of the values of public duty. Indeed, the very term "civil servant" has a strong sense of the values attached to public service. However, value-based leadership has a wider sense than that of the common values of public service implicit in traditional public agencies. Value-based leadership (as described in Chapter 6) has the following characteristics:

1. Those exercising leadership must have personal values consistent with the values of the organization. Those exercising leadership must have a high ethical standard.
2. Those exercising leadership must be true to their own values.

The book does not immediately take the reader to the concept of value-based leadership. Rather, we commence by considering the nature of professions and values. The public sector is a highly professionalized domain and this is a key starting point.

Therefore we show the reader that in order to work with value-based leadership, insights into the universe of values surrounding professional organizations in the public sector are needed. Leadership must always be adapted to the specificities of the present context.

Part 1 of the book first provides an introduction to what characterizes the professions and professional organizations. Then, a thorough review of the values in public professions is presented. Here, the emphasis is placed on public values, professional values, professional ethics, and professional identity. Finally, an introduction to the more general theory of values is presented. This is necessary if one is to identify the values within one's own organization.

Part 2 of the book then moves on to examine leadership in a value-based context. Value-based leadership is not just about working with the values. It is also necessary to focus on the leadership function. Therefore, values must be integrated with the leadership processes and directed towards realizing important goals. Part 2 first contains a brief introduction to the development of leadership theory and then moves on to parse out a conceptual model for value-based leadership. Here, the first emphasis is on showing how leadership can be anchored in a solid value base. Part 2 ends by reviewing the various methods that can be used to work with value development. Here, we will also discuss whether it is desirable to change employees' values, and how leaders should handle conflicting values in their own organizations.

Finally, having established the theoretical basis for values and leadership in Part 3, we conclude by moving onto the practice of value-based leadership. Thus, in the last part of the book, the purpose is to show how this type of leadership can be used in practice. Firstly we introduce the concept of self-leadership, which is a crucial form of leadership in all professional work. Secondly we look at team leadership, which is a common form of leadership in public professions. Finally we evaluate transformational leadership. This leadership form has a clear value base, and thus appears as a value-based supplement to other, more traditional forms of leadership at the organizational level.

The pedagogical approach throughout the book is to furnish the reader with learning points at the outset of each chapter and to offer a mixture of generic and concrete examples throughout to illustrate the concepts. At the end of each chapter we also provide a number of short exercises for the reader to explore and develop their understanding of the concepts together with a focused amount of further reading.

TOR BUSCH
Professor Emeritus
Trondheim Business School
Norway

ALEX MURDOCK
Professor of Not for Profit Management and Leadership
London South Bank University, UK

Introduction

Key learning points

At the end of this chapter the reader should be able to:

- understand the basic perspectives of value-based leadership
- be aware of the special characteristics of the public sector
- be aware of the major changes that have taken place in the public sector during the last 30 years.

Values have always played a central role in the public sector – as a public ethos among employees in public administration, or as an important platform for employees in public professions. An important function of values in this context is that they contribute to the organization's social legitimacy. Organizations that live up to the values of wider society become bearers of values in their own right, and as such they are held in high esteem. As well as creating high social legitimacy, values also contribute to high quality in service production. Public values ensure that employees do what is right based on their own conviction, thus reducing the need for control systems. The objective of this book is to integrate the values held within public-sector professions with relevant leadership theories – thus, the three main perspectives addressed are: a leadership perspective, a value perspective, and a public perspective.

1.1 A leadership perspective

In a book on value-based leadership it is important to focus on the leadership process. Leadership is regarded by many as a complex and complicated

1

phenomenon, and it has a relatively short history as an independent discipline. Furthermore, no simple, well-established, coherent paradigm is dominant within leadership research. There are many theories, emphasizing different dimensions of leadership.

In this book we have decided to choose a process-oriented leadership theory, which emphasizes that leadership takes place on all organizational levels. In this theoretical perspective, the focus is on the leadership process rather than the individual leader. According to this theory, leadership behaviour is a form of human behaviour in its own right. It is disconnected from the leader as an individual, and can be conducted by any individual present in an organization – irrespective of whether they are managers, staff members, or representatives of other stakeholders in the coalition. Thus, all professional employees engage in leadership as part of their job. Leadership is not exercised all of the time, but is implicit when goals are to be set, and when good results are to be attained.

According to this theory, leadership is defined as a goal-setting, problem-solving, and language-creating interaction between relevant persons (Johnsen, 2006). First of all, a basic requirement is a clear focus on the organization's goals. Goals must be interpreted and reformulated to ensure that they are always relevant in relation to the tasks to be solved. Second, a good problem-solving ability must be developed. Setting good goals is not enough; the leadership must also result in the realization of these goals. Third, leaders and staff must be able to communicate with each other. A shared set of concepts or a shared language adapted to the challenges faced by the organization must be developed. Finally, good interaction must be developed between all of those who conduct leadership. The different individuals must be able to understand each other, also, on an emotional level. Relationships based on trust must be developed in the organization, both horizontally and vertically.

1.2   A value perspective

Value-based leadership requires a clear focus on the values that are present in the organization – which is captured by the concept of organizational culture. In studying organizational culture, three perspectives can be used (Schultz, 1995). First of all, we can take a *rational perspective* as our starting point. According to this perspective, organizational culture is a useful tool in the creation of well-functioning organizations, and much effort is spent on developing a normative value platform for staff behaviour. There is great emphasis on creating a shared organizational culture. Different subcultures existing within the organization are perceived as undesirable. In that they are regarded as deviations from the preferred culture, subcultures are often defined as a problem.

Secondly, organizational culture can be considered from a *functional perspective*. Here the culture of an organization is regarded as the result of a long process: the values develop as a function of the organization solving its tasks and finding its place in society. Only the most functional values survive this process – namely the values that help the organization meet the stakeholders' expectations. In the public sector, the main stakeholders are users, staff, higher authorities, and politicians. Organizational culture is not easily altered according to this perspective. As a response to the challenges it has faced over time, the culture of an organization is relatively stable. Since the external challenges encountered by different organizational units are not uniform, the emergence of organizational subcultures is seen as a natural part of the process.

Finally, organizational culture can be considered in a *symbolic perspective*, which puts the focus on the meaning attributed to different aspects of the organization. When an action acquires symbolic significance it means that it expresses something beyond the content of the concrete action. For example, a primary school might decide that every morning teachers must shake the young students' hands. Symbolic significance associated with respect for the students, and seeing each and every individual, can be attributed to this ritual. Thus, for students and parents as well as teachers, the action takes on a wider significance than the hand-shaking as such.

From this perspective, the culture of an organization is a shared pattern of interpretation. The existence of a shared interpretation of reality among its employees creates strong cohesion with the organization – it gives a perception of shared identity. Organizational culture cannot be explained as a matter of cause and effect. It emerges through social interaction involving constant interpretation and re-interpretation of reality. Subcultures are explained as expressions of the co-existence of different patterns of interpretation within the same organization, and individuals can also alternate between such patterns depending on the situation. Consequently, organizational culture emerges as less clear-cut than in the other perspectives. Different groups within the same organization can interpret the same action in different ways.

The main emphasis in this book is on the functional perspective. Thus we take as our starting point that the values of a given organization have developed over a long period of time, and also that they reflect value development in society at large. We regard dominant values in society, in any given organization, and in any given profession as stable over time. Thus implementing major cultural changes in an organization is a difficult undertaking. At the same time, drawing on a rational perspective can also become necessary. We consider it important to be able to discuss what values are desirable in an organization. Finally, we also attribute some weight to the symbolic perspective. Open processes allow neglected values to be brought into focus. Changing existing values is not always necessary: adjusting their meaning might be enough.

The distinctive features of the public professions also provide important frameworks for value-based leadership practices. Public professions are held in high esteem in society at large, and represent fundamental values shared by the population. Common for all the professions is the members' wide latitude of discretion. Professionals are often faced with problems, which require that they make quick decisions based on experience and competence. Even if they are not employed in leadership positions, the nature of their work requires a large amount of discretion. Hence, rather than attempting to control or monitor individual decisions, the organizations focus on quality assurance in respect of the staff members' values and level of competence.

Value-based leadership involving public-sector professions must be based on the distinguishing features of these professions, the professional organizations, and the professionals involved. School or hospital leadership is different in significant respects from leading a manufacturing company or a commercial firm. The expertise of professional employees has been built over a long period of time, and is largely tacit. It has developed through practice, enabling the professional to gradually master the art of rapidly coping with complicated and complex problems as soon as they emerge. Without deep insight into the distinctive qualities of the profession involved, value-based leadership is virtually impossible.

1.3   A public perspective

Although leadership and management entail elements that are general and therefore legitimate in both private and public organizations, the leadership must be adapted to the particular organization. Value-based leadership in public professions must therefore be adjusted to the characteristics present in the public sector.

The overall goals and values are important in this context. Within public administration, key objectives are linked to welfare, social equity, and justice. Mark Moore stimulated the debate about these goals by introducing the concept of public value (Moore, 1995). In 2010, Bennington and Moore revisited the concept with a focus upon the theory and practice of public value. The key issue for leadership is the importance of public managers considering the outcomes for the wider public stakeholder interest (Bennington and Moore, 2010). This may mean a trade-off against other management priorities such as efficiency and minimizing the cost of services provided. Leadership also involves a close awareness of the political dimension and the importance of building coalitions in order to achieve outcomes for the benefit not just of clients but also citizens and the community in general. This lays emphasis upon the need for public leaders to reframe questions in a way which might be addressed through the engagement of civic groups and civil society organizations. This requires, on the part of public managers, a sensitivity to values held by these groups and organizations.

A major challenge with public goals arises from the difficulty of measuring results. At a school, these measures can be converted into more specific goals on class environment, development of knowledge, social development, and care. Although these goals are seen as important, they are difficult to quantify. Measuring results is therefore a problem, or at least a challenge in most public organizations. Another challenge is that the goals in the public sector are often vague, ambiguous, conflicting, and unstable. They depend on political processes, and new political priorities or new constellations can lead to rapid changes.

The process of problem-solving is also different in the public sector. Achieving legitimacy means that many groups must be heard in the political process. Although democratic processes can be time-consuming, they are also valuable and important to protect. We would not necessarily remove democracy and participation to improve efficiency; democracy is a key institution and thus a value in itself. In this context, leadership and management necessarily have different characteristics compared to private enterprises. For example, building a new school is considered a relatively simple task. Based on a given budget and specific requirements for the school's design, the task is defined as technical and economic in nature. And it can usually easily be solved by providing the necessary expertise. But when carried out in the public sector, building a new school is not so simple. A politically driven discussion on where the school should be located and how it should be designed can easily arise. Perhaps the investment will be compared to alternative ways of using the public resources, such as constructing a new nursing home or improving the safety of a road that the children use when walking to school. Hence, complex political processes emerge and can lead to major delays, even though the need for the school is clear and the financing is available.

The production of services to the population is not necessarily a major distinction between private and public institutions. However, the public sector has the responsibility for supplying an extended product (Klausen, 1996). A school should not only ensure that students acquire desirable skills; students should also be socialized to certain social values. Social services are not only designed to take care of people who are in a difficult situation; they also serve to reflect the welfare state's values., This means that professional employees are expected to recognize and aspire to some superior and complex goals which are difficult to transfer to the lives of specific individuals. Physicians, for example, should not only treat individual patients; they should also help develop a good state of health in the population. Moreover, the professions are given the responsibility for demonstrating key values in society so that our political system and social welfare services achieve a good reputation among the population. This is not always easy in a situation where politicians are reducing the resource base, requiring higher productivity, or implementing comprehensive reforms.

Public institutions are also subject to special conditions. First, they rarely operate in market systems. With few exceptions, public administration produces goods and services for society without specific considerations of direct payment by the recipient. This means that it is not possible to measure the value added in the same way as private companies measure sales revenues. Politicians are the ones who ultimately decide whether the services have a high enough value compared to the resources consumed when producing them. Although politicians can base their decision on user inputs, expert analysis, and other information, there is always a significant degree of discretion. The ultimate judge is the voter whereas with the market the ultimate judge is the consumer or purchaser.

A second condition is that the operations of public institutions are largely regulated by rules, laws, and ordinances, which in turn reduces the freedom in leadership decision making and affects the kind of leadership and management that can be exercised. When these conditions are properly instituted, the potential for corruption is small and the resources are appropriately allocated to the intended service. At the same time, the political system is also partly characterized by low levels of predictability, which creates problems for long-term planning. Shifting political coalitions can rapidly, sometimes literally "overnight," change the essential conditions for the organization and financing of welfare production.

Therefore, leadership and management in public institutions require insights into a multitude of different dimensions, and there is a need for a conceptual framework that equally includes the political and cultural reality as well as the economic reality (Melander, 1997). The reality of ambiguity, conflicting objectives, power, and political activity, along with the instrumental rationality must be acknowledged. In the public sector there is a constant challenge from other norms of rationality that can have equal or greater legitimacy among key stakeholders.

Developments within the public sector during the last 30 years have been part of an international trend – namely New Public Management (NPM) – where the public sector has been heavily shaped by a variety of models from the private sector (Pollitt and Bouckaert, 2011). This includes a greater emphasis on competition and performance measures, a stronger focus on the users and stronger governance, and an increased prevalence of concepts like accountability. Yet after a thorough assessment, the OECD (2005) concludes that the reforms are context-dependent, and transferring leadership techniques from the private to the public sector has proven to be difficult. Context dependency has resulted in many of the NPM reforms having different effects in different countries. Instead of adding general managerial and market principles as a basis for reform, the OECD recommended that all changes should be made on a case-by-case basis. Although adequate evaluations are lacking, the conclusion is that the reforms conducted over recent years have led to greater transparency, greater efficiency, stronger user orientation, and greater focus on results in most OECD countries. The extent of change should not be overstated, and in many countries, reforms have not lived up to the expectations of them.

While many of the NPM-inspired changes have become institutionalized, the limitations of this concept are increasingly obvious regarding solutions to key challenges in the public sector. It is therefore argued that today, a stronger focus on leadership and the leadership concept, rather than on governance among key political actors, is more suitable for handling the complexity within the public sector (Brookes & Grint, 2010). This is consistent with the growing criticism of NPM from a network perspective. A key argument here is that the NPM has led to greater fragmentation of the public sector and reduced the ability to find holistic solutions (Christensen & Lægreid, 2007).

Another criticism is linked to NPM's rather weak emphasis on the basis of value in the public sector (Beck-Jørgensen & Vrangbæk, 2004; Christensen & Lægreid, 2007; Olsen, 2007). In the public sector, there has always been a strong focus on values, and the most crucial dimensions are captured by the concept of a public ethos (Lundquist, 1991). In addition, professional values play a central role – especially in connection with public service. Today's growing focus on values in the public sector indicates the possibility of strengthening the legitimacy of professional influence. This indicates that in the future we may see an increased focus on norms and values in the public sector – that is, greater emphasis on value-based leadership.

> ### Exercises for further development and understanding
>
> - Try to describe a leader whom you are familiar with – write down all the dimensions you can think of. To what extent are these dimensions related to goal-setting, problem-solving, language-creating, and interaction?
> - Picture an organization that you are familiar with. Describe three values that according to you are present in this organization. Give a rational, a functional, and a symbolic explanation for why these values exist in the organization.
> - Picture an organization that you are familiar with, or use your knowledge about the public sector and describe some of the changes that have taken place during the last 10–20 years. Which of these changes do you consider being part of the New Public Management?

Recommended further reading

Christensen, T. & Lægreid, P. (eds) (2007). *Transcending New Public Management: The Transformation of Public Sector Reforms*. Aldershot: Ashgate.

Pollitt, C. & Bouckaert, G. (2011). *Public Management Reform: A Comparative Analysis – New Public Management, Governance and the Neo-Weberian State*. Oxford: Oxford University Press.

Part 1
Professions and values

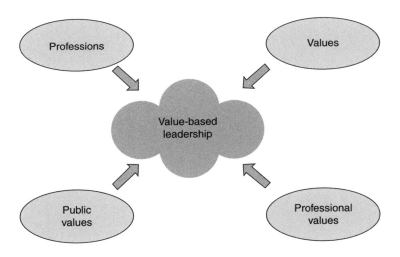

In order to work with value-based leadership, insights into the universe of values surrounding professional organizations in the public sector are needed. Leadership must always be adapted to the specificities of the present context. Part 1 of the book first provides an introduction to what characterizes the professions and professional organizations. Then a thorough review of the values in public professions is presented. Here, the emphasis is placed on public values, professional values, professional ethics, and professional identity. Finally, an introduction to the more general theory of values is presented. This is necessary if one is to identify the values within one's own organization.

Professionalism theory

2

Key learning points

At the end of this chapter the reader should be able to:

- have an understanding of the nature of professions and the theoretical basis which underpins this understanding
- appreciate the importance of the concepts of expertise, specialism, and competence and the way they are utilized to both define and protect the entry, boundaries, and regulation which determines a profession
- be able to apply these concepts in both an organizational and an individual context
- be aware of how professional progression operates and the way that links to both knowledge acquisition and demonstration
- understand the differences between bureaucratic, business, and professional rationalities.

This book is about the leadership of professional workers. So, what does professional mean within this context? In everyday language, the term "professional" is often used to describe an individual with a high level of competence in a particular field. In this book, we will narrow down this definition and make the assumption that a professional practitioner is a person who belongs to a particular profession. Furthermore, we focus on those professions that are dominant in the public sector. If we are to discuss the leadership of professional employees, we first need to know more about what characterizes the professions. Are there any similarities between the professions in the public sector – whether they be related to health, education, social services, police, defence, or other professional occupations? In what follows, we take a look at what characterizes the professions, the professional organizations, and the professional employees. Each of these characteristics may affect what form of leadership is most suitable – or needed.

2.1   What characterizes the professions?

Traditional professions, such as the medical profession and the legal profession, have a long history and have always had a high level of status within society. They represent important vocational competences, have gained a central position in society, and exhibit major influences on their own disciplines. At the end of the 20th century, there was an increasing number of new "professions," and various occupational groups worked hard to achieve a professional status. This development of the professions takes place over several phases (Wilensky, 1964). In a first phase, the goal is to form a full-time working group of individuals with specialized skills. Next, educational institutions must be established and take responsibility for education and professional development. Finally, the professional workers and the employees of educational institutions must organize to take control of the profession and protect themselves against competition from others. Therefore, there are two main goals in this process. The first goal is to obtain professional control of a particular field of work or activity (Freidson, 2001). This means that the profession establishes control over the content and methods of the occupation. The second goal is to control entry to the profession so that only people with a specific education have access to it as a source of employment (Abbott, 1988). This means that the professional practitioners can govern themselves without being subjected to significant influences from the external environment (Noordegraaf, 2007). Increased professionalization of occupations has therefore changed the balance of power within society, which has led to greater societal scepticism towards and concern about a profession's ability to exercise control over its professional domain.

So, what characterizes an ideal profession? While there is no definitive answer to this question, we can highlight some dimensions that will normally be present in an ideal profession (Freidson, 2001):

1. The profession represents specialized expertise.
2. The profession has exclusive control over a defined field.
3. The profession is protected in the labour market.
4. The profession is based on a specific form of higher education.
5. The profession is based on an ideology that focuses on quality.

We could argue that an ideal profession should fulfil all five of these dimensions. The question then is whether or not it is useful to distinguish between professions and non-professions. Perhaps it is better to talk about degrees of professionalism. The "pure" professions will fulfil all the dimensions, while new professions may only fulfil some of them. We will now look more closely at what these five dimensions entail.

The profession represents specialized expertise

Professionalism is about the competence-related content of a profession, where competence in this case emphasizes knowledge and skills. Knowledge represents a theoretical understanding of how specific tasks within the profession should be performed. By contrast, skills are the ability to perform a certain task in practice. A nurse must be able to administer injections, a physical therapist must be able to massage, and a police officer must be able to calm down aggressive people. Professionals can acquire theoretical knowledge through study; however, skills are also developed through practice. To some degree, a profession will also expect or require specific abilities or personal qualities. As such, some professional education not only subjects applicants to formal qualifications, but might also test applicants for specific abilities. For example, applicants for police positions are tested with respect to both physical and mental abilities. In other professions, students will be examined for their suitability before being certified as eligible for the profession – as has happened with teachers. In addition to these formal requirements, a form of self-selection will also take place. Potential applicants will be attracted to careers in which they think of themselves as suitable to practise. People who are empathetic and caring, for example, may prefer occupations where such attributes are valued.

In addition to being specialized, the profession's knowledge base must also consist of a theoretical foundation (Freidson, 2001). In practice, this means that professional knowledge must be research-based, and theoretical models that set the elements of professional knowledge into a larger context must be developed. Thus, theoretical knowledge makes it possible to obtain fundamental insights that bridge the different skills and make it easier to evaluate and acquire new skills. While a specific skill can be short-lived, a theoretical insight can at all times be adjusted in relation to the development of knowledge within a discipline.

The basis of competence must be formalized at least in part – that is, it can be described and communicated in a training situation. The complexity must also be sufficient to require a significant amount of time for skills to be developed. Many of the required competences must also be of a kind that cannot be described or formalized (Noordegraaf, 2007). This means that it will not always be possible to establish a set of rules for how a task should be performed. The reason for this is that within professional occupations, the workers will face unusual or unexpected situations. A physician, for example, will encounter patients with abnormal personalities and histories of illness, a police officer must be able to handle a dangerous and complex situation, and a teacher will meet different classes that have their own particular dynamics. Therefore, professionals must be able to apply judgements and choose a procedure they think is suitable in the prevailing situation. This type of skill takes a long time to develop, and it is primarily developed through practice. Moreover, much of this expertise can be described as tacit knowledge (Polanyi, 1974) – that is, the professional workers are not conscious of the knowledge-based foundation for their actions. When a child welfare consultant is facing a particularly challenging family, she or he will intuitively choose words and actions on the basis of the process that takes place. It is like riding a bike – once you have learned it, you do not continue to think about how to do it. The tasks performed in professional occupations have therefore a high degree of complexity; they require both knowledge and skills, many of which are tacit and largely entail the exercise of judgement. This means that the tasks of the profession can rarely be performed by persons who lack formal education or training in the profession backed up with actual experience of carrying out professional activities.

If we analyse the tasks of the professional workers, we will see that high levels of competence are not necessary in all situations. Some of the tasks are easy to perform and open up the possibility of challenging the hegemony of the profession. Teachers have assistants, auxiliary nurses take over some of the tasks performed by nurses, and security guards have taken over some of the tasks formerly performed by police officers. The reason for these takeovers can be a shortage of professional labour or lower labour costs. While these changes are not critical for the professions, they do indicate that the areas of expertise within professions may be in a state of flux.

The profession has exclusive control over a defined field

Another important feature of the professions is found in their control over their particular fields of expertise. This control covers three factors: job content, horizontal specialization, and vertical specialization. A large portion of this control is exercised through negotiations between the profession and representatives from public authorities (Freidson, 2001). Control over job content means that the profession will be the predominant influence in deciding which methods and professional standards will be applied to the field. Within the medical profession, for example, this knowledge will partly be developed through actually practising medicine and partly through conducting relevant research. Therefore doctors will be constantly confronted with changes, as new methods are developed and implemented. This applies generally to professions. New technology and new knowledge tends to challenge the prevailing methods, and some professions may therefore come under intense pressure and experience a rapid pace of change. Other professions may be more conservative, and the implementation of new methods may take longer in these cases. Usually the choice of method is made by the professional workers. Indeed, the high level of complexity within many professions makes it difficult for outsiders to intervene in this process.

In reality, the choices made within the professions will be subject to pressure, and in many professions the government can push to change the professional practice. For example, the education directorate can legislate guidelines regarding which priorities should be implemented in schools. They can collect experience from abroad and they can implement a new education policy. Even if the teachers' organizations are involved in the process, they may have no control over the guidelines drawn up for the education policy. We will find similar types of pressure in most public professions. An expertise is built up within the bureaucracy, which in certain situations will challenge the profession's influence on how the job should be conducted. This can be formalized through laws, regulations, or specific directives. Among other things, we have experienced the development of stronger regulative and market management in the public-sector professions (Broadbent & Raughlin, 2007), including the growth of various forms of quality-assurance systems, requirements that certain procedures be followed, and new reporting systems. This development has reduced the professions' opportunities to choose their own methods and has undermined their traditional forms of control.

Horizontal specialization describes the extent of established specialized areas in a profession. Within the education profession, for example, there are few areas of specialization at the elementary level. Here, most teachers can teach across a range of subjects. At the intermediate level, there is an increase in the number of specialized areas, where teachers focus on certain subjects. At the highest educational level, the teachers may focus even further. We can see something similar within the healthcare system. Nurses and doctors working in the initial medical situations are typically generalists, while doctors and nurses in specialist hospitals may be focused on particular medical needs such as children or mental health. With the increasing complexity of tasks, we thus obtain a greater degree of horizontal specialization. When the professions are in control of horizontal specialization, it is often the professionals themselves who decide on how many specialties will be established within the profession. For a specialization to be functional, it must be possible to find an acceptable solution within the specialization. When a hospital employs a doctor who specializes in the ear, nose, and throat, then most referrals in these areas should be treated by him or her without the need to consult with other specialists. Normally, patients assessed for specialist treatment should be allocated to one of the specialized units when they are admitted to the hospital. Possessing such appropriate specialization requires a high level of professional competence in the particular area of work.

The last factor is vertical specialization, which consists of the distribution of tasks between the different levels of hierarchy within an organization. Hence, the relevant question here is which and how many levels of management will be established above those who work in daily production. For example, how many layers of management should there be between a police officer and the chief of police in a given region? The professions have had an influence here too, although not as much as their influence in job content and horizontal specialization. Some professions have a pronounced degree of vertical specialization – for example, within uniformed services such as the army. Other professions, by contrast, have flatter hierarchies and a lesser degree of vertical specialization.

We contend that professions typically maintain strong control over their work content and degree of specialization. Changes require professional knowledge, and it is only the professionals who can make these decisions. However, research also shows that the professionals are challenged by political authorities who feel they have insufficient force of control, or by suspicions that professional employees are not loyal enough in relation to the overarching management of the organization (see Busch & Dehlin, 2011 for review).

Example 1

Social work as a profession

Social work is nowadays found in most countries and is regarded generally as a professional activity with training based at universities. It is typically regulated with both national and international recognition. How did this come about? The origins are generally seen in 19th-century England and the USA coming from a mixture of concerns around poverty and migration. It was often linked to faith-based organizations and gradually came to be increasingly part of the public sector with social workers being employed by the state or by state agencies.

The growth of government regulation and a general perception that the government should accept a responsibility to intervene in a wider range of social problems has extended the remit of social work beyond its origins with poverty. Specialization in areas such as childcare, mental health and disability, and the challenges of old age have emerged together with specialism around particular forms of intervention and practice. In the UK now, the term "social worker" is restricted to those who have undertaken and passed a recognized training (usually to Master's level) and who have complied with registration requirements. There are regulatory mechanisms to police the profession and expectations that social workers will update their practice during their working career.

These professional developments are increasingly found across other countries.

The profession is protected in the labour market

In a free labour market, employers can hire the people they believe are best qualified. In such a situation, the applicant's education and experience are given considerable weight. This provides assurances for individuals with a specialized education that they will obtain the jobs they are educated to do. This is especially important in those jobs that have a large degree of flexibility in how tasks are conducted, and where it is also difficult for managers to control the quality of the tasks. In these situations, we often have a form of control based on the standardization of skills (Mintzberg, 1983), which entails the construction of standardized requirements for the kinds of knowledge that workers should have.

Within the public-sector professions, standardization translates into employment based upon specific educational requirements. In practice, this usually means that to be hired as a doctor, lawyer or teacher, etc., applicants must have an accredited higher education for the state to ensure that those working within these professions have adequate expertise. Thus, strong institutions (rules of action) are established which give professionals a protected status in the labour market. For example, the regulations promulgated by the legislation of most countries in the EU include a description of what education is required for teachers to be able to teach at the various levels of the school system. Similar regulations are found in other professions. With these requirements, we can say that the professions have acquired a level of institutional power that gives them control over the selection of candidates competing for vacant positions. This is partly achieved through negotiations between the government and the professions, and partly through conflicts with competing professions (Freidson, 2001). An example is found in people who work in preschool education, experience of which is now sometimes accepted as the basis for teaching at the primary school level. In such a case, the general teacher profession has lost its former monopoly over teaching in these grades. In the UK there has been a government initiative which enables graduates with good degrees to start as teachers at both primary and secondary school level without having undertaken and passed a teaching diploma.

Protection in the labour market not only affects employment, but also affects career advancement within the profession. The most common career path in public professions can be described as horizontal. This means that a person advances in his or her career without moving into a senior managerial position. Through increased knowledge, it is possible to achieve a higher reputation and professional status – often combined with higher wages. For example, at the university level, we find a variety of professional positions that require a special combination of education and documented research. The regulations governing employment in these positions have been prepared in collaboration with representatives from the affected professions. For a specific type of university employment, the quality of the applicants may also be evaluated by a committee of faculty members from several universities. Thus, this profession has participated in the development of the regulations while its members assess who meets the academic requirements for employment. In other words, this profession maintains a very powerful position in the labour market.

The profession is based on a specific form of higher education

As previously described, eligibility in a professional career typically requires a special type of education. For some professions – such as the medical profession – education has come to be associated with an academic education. This has helped to give the profession a high academic status. In many other professions, the education requirements were set to a lower academic level and were to a larger extent more skill-oriented. Developments over the last 40 years have shown that most professional education increasingly takes place in the college or university system. This has resulted in a strong academization of professional education (Kyvik, 2009) and a stronger emphasis on research.

This development has provided the professions with a stronger position in society. In addition to having gained an academic status, they have also gained greater influence on the development of knowledge within their own field of expertise. Moreover, most employees within higher professional education also belong to the profession itself, and to a large extent systematic research allows them to set the premises for the field's development. The research provides greater insights into complex problem areas and contributes to the development of new professional standards. These insights are then imparted to the students, who in turn bring updated knowledge into the practical professional work. In addition to the basic education that qualifies students for employment, we also see a growth in the availability of additional education, which can be directed towards a specialization within the profession or towards qualifications for managerial positions.

In addition to imparting knowledge and skills, educational institutions will also contribute to greater awareness of the profession's culture and identity among the students. Central values and ethical rules are included in the lectures, so that the profession emerges with a clear portfolio of shared values. In this way, educational institutions also contribute to students experiencing the profession as a unified entity. Hence, socialization into the profession begins well before the students start their practice. This is reinforced when students are allowed to become student members of the membership body of their relevant professions. For example, all police students may join the Police Association, all nursing students can join the Nurses' Association, and all teacher students can join the Teachers' Association.

The profession is based on an ideology that focuses on quality

The last dimension pertains to the particular ideological and value-based foundation of the profession (Freidson, 2001). More specifically, professional practitioners have a greater commitment to doing a good job rather than obtaining personal financial gain. Furthermore, professionals are more concerned with quality than with efficiency. These are values that are anchored in society, and these values will strengthen the profession's legitimacy. By appearing as carriers of core values, the professions achieve a strong institutional status. They appear valuable and obtain strong support among the population, although it can be rather hard to assess the impact of their efforts. Their specialization also contributes to a high degree of legitimacy in part because, in our Western society, specialization is a characteristic associated with economic development, and it is expected that high rates of specialization lead to higher levels of productivity and quality. This also serves the professions. Therefore, the core values of the professions are important for their legitimacy in society, and extensive efforts are taken in order to develop the basis for these values and ethical guidelines. This is of great importance for a value-based leadership of professionals, and we will therefore expand into the professions' core values in a later chapter.

These five points indicate that a profession can be described by using several of the dimensions. Theoretically, we can envisage an ideal profession as one that receives full scores on all dimensions. However, this is not how it works in reality. There is after all no such thing as an ideal profession, and public-sector professions, as opposed to professions in the private sector, will score differently if they are analysed according to these dimensions. Moreover, the professions are in a constant state of flux. Some of them achieve a stronger professional basis, while others are losing the battle against the government and against competing professions.

2.2   What characterizes professional organizations?

The characteristics of professions will significantly shape the professional organizations in the public sector – whether it is the police force, defence, the education sector, or other sizeable public service areas. This was especially studied by Henry Mintzberg (1983), who referred to such organizations as professional bureaucracies. He uses this term deliberately to highlight both their large proportion of professional workers and their strong bureaucratic characteristics. The bureaucratic characteristics in professional bureaucracies are not tied to the traditional, formal structures that exist in what he calls machine bureaucracies. Instead, the characteristics are tied to the presence of professional standards that, in his opinion, may be just as bureaucratic as formal rules. In other words, the methods developed within the various professions to a large degree govern the behaviour of the professional employees. So, what characterizes a professional bureaucracy? The characteristic can be summarized, following Mintzberg (1983) as follows:

1. Main focus on service production
2. High degree of decentralization
3. High degree of specialization
4. Controlled by formal requirements for worker qualifications.

Let us now take a closer look at these points.

Main focus on service production

This means that the dominant group of employees works with the production of services for users. If we take a closer look at a school, a hospital, or a children's welfare office, we will see that most employees work directly with students, patients, or clients. The activity is centred on public welfare production and is in contrast to public administration, where most workers handle case processing or manage the exercise of authority. Therefore, a professional bureaucracy will largely be evaluated on its ability to produce good services, even though the demand for efficiency has increased in recent years.

High degree of decentralization

Decentralization means decision-making authority has moved far down in the organization. In practice, this means that professional workers have been given wide latitude, autonomy, and discretion in their work. For example, a teacher will largely determine how courses are organized. A professional bureaucracy is thus characterized by a large number of workers with professional backgrounds who have considerable authority to exercise judgements in their jobs. In some professional organizations, members have also had the authority to elect or appoint their professional managers.

High degree of specialization

The professions themselves are specialized, and this is carried through by the specialization of professional workers. The degree of specialization depends on the specific requirements of the job. In a hospital with highly specialized tasks, we therefore find a strong level of specialization among the professional staff, including doctors, nurses, and other professional groups. For example, after completing medical studies, all doctors begin to work in a specialized area. Some concentrate on medicine in the community while others become surgeons in hospitals. At larger hospitals, we find an even greater level of specialization within these areas. Moreover, the fact that professionals often work alone can be seen as another form of specialization. A teacher is alone with his or her students most of the time – in the same way that the social worker will meet with his or her clients without having colleagues present. Another feature is that the work usually starts with a *diagnosis*. It is this diagnosis that determines the measures to be used. The professional's expertise therefore lies in the ability to both make a good diagnosis and choose the best treatment or activity in the light of that diagnosis.

Controlled by requirements for worker qualifications

There are several ways of managing an organization, and we can distinguish between management in the form of direct supervision and management in the form of standardization (Mintzberg, 1983). When it comes to the latter, we can further distinguish between standardization of work processes, standardization of output (performance management), and standardization of skills. The final form is typically found in professional bureaucracies, where control is derived from employees satisfying specific educational requirements. The reasons behind this are:

- The work is performed in direct contact with users, and the professionals have a large degree of flexibility in work performance. Thus, it is difficult for others to exercise direct supervision over the work.
- In the face of a wide latitude for discretion, it is difficult to design a set of rules for how the job should be done. Therefore, there is little scope for standardization of work processes.
- It is difficult to adequately measure the results of the work. The work that is carried out is complex, and the results depend on a variety of conditions that the professionals are unable to influence. Therefore, there is little scope for standardization of output.

Standardization of skills is thus the key form of management that can be easily implemented in professional organizations. For the standardization of skills to operate adequately, the organization must have competent and conscientious workers, and this is not always the case. Problems can arise when a large scope for discretion allows employees the possibility of ignoring the interests of users, colleagues, and the organization itself (Mintzberg, 1983).

According to Mintzberg (1983), discretion can cause other actors in the organization's environment to feel that there is insufficient external control over professionals and their organizations. The result is a pressure on professional organizations to implement other forms of governance. This is well documented in the public sector (Broadbent & Laughlin, 2002). The problem is that other forms of governance can result in significant dysfunctions. In other words, they can create adverse side effects. For example, standardization of work processes can reduce the professional's ability to utilize her specific expertise. Under this kind of management, he or she must now follow bureaucratic rules rather than her own judgement, possibly resulting in a decline in the service's quality. Moreover, using performance-based management can shift the focus to areas that are easier to measure, while areas that are difficult to measure are simply neglected. An example of this has been advanced as measurement of school teachers' performance by the results of standardized pupil tests. This leads some teachers to assert that a strong emphasis on student achievements in standardized tests has a negative effect on the overall quality of the schools.

In practice, we find both standardization of work processes and output in all professional organizations. However, it is important to note that these forms of management have obvious limitations. This is the reason why a strong focus on organizational culture is emphasized as an essential form of governance in predominantly professional organizations (Ouchi, 1979). This contributes to a form of self-leadership that may function effectively in situations where it is difficult to establish rules and hard to measure the results.

2.3   What characterizes professional employees?

Those who work in professional occupations will naturally be influenced by the norms of the professions to which they belong. They have a special type of education, they have a job with sizeable scope for discretion, and they usually identify themselves with the professional culture and professional identity. Let us now consider two dimensions that are important in conjunction with the leadership of professional employees.

The first dimension is the professional development from a beginner to an expert (Dreyfus, Dreyfus & Athanasiou, 1988). Here is a description of the five stages of professional development:

1. Beginner
2. Advanced beginner

3. Competent practitioner
4. Skilled practitioner
5. Expert.

This development can be described as moving up a staircase – reaching a new step of competence on each level. In a beginner phase, the professionals will largely depend on their theoretical knowledge. Through formal education, they have learned in principle to make a diagnosis and have acquired classroom-based knowledge of what methods should be used. However, they have little training in how to do this in practice. In most professional occupations, learning the practice begins during formal education, where students are allowed to solve problems in real tasks under the guidance of a skilled practitioner or an expert. A student teacher, for example, will attend class for the first time and have to deal with individual students, the classroom environment, and academic challenges. The experience will be discussed with an experienced teacher, and the student begins the long journey to become an expert. After the first faltering steps, the beginners achieve more confidence, and they learn to cope with various challenges in conducting their work. Then they arrive at a more advanced level and are able to find practical solutions that are tailored to each situation they face. However, they can still be knocked off balance when they encounter unfamiliar problems. Eventually, they evolve to become a competent practitioner, where they have learned to recognize the situations they encounter and will intuitively select the methods that worked in previous situations.

Research has shown that, when compared to novices, experts spend more time studying the problem and less time solving it. Experts transfer the problem to an abstract form and classify it as a particular type. Once this is done, a cognitive map relevant to the issue is gathered together. The major difference between experts and beginners seems to lie in the number of cognitive maps on hand and the size of these maps (Chase & Simon, 1973; Chi, Feltowich & Glaser, 1981; Chi, Glaser & Rees, 1982). Therefore, in the evolution from beginner to expert, a professional practitioner will first of all develop a large number of cognitive maps which makes it possible to recognize a situation. These cognitive maps or mental models will also contain information on what actions worked in previous situations. An expert will thus be able to quickly make appropriate decisions on what needs to be done. This applies to all professional employees. Second, an expert has a greater ability to see the principles of the situation, thus making it easier to analyse a problem at hand. This does not mean that all professionals will become experts, but over time they will develop a specific set of competencies in actions that enable them to handle the challenges of the job.

From the perspective of leadership styles, it is of significant importance for leaders to know where in this development process a professional employee is (Hersey & Blanchard, 1977). Beginners will often appear as immature co-workers who have difficulty handling the job – which creates uncertainty among beginners. In these situations, it is important to have a leader who can help steer the beginner's behaviour. This means that the leader gives clear guidelines on how the job should be performed. This will create greater confidence and reduce the possibility that something will go wrong. As the employee becomes more mature and leaves the beginner stage, it is recommended that the leader reduce her tendency to steer and shift instead to providing support for the employee's efforts in developing his own skills. As maturity increases further, the leader should reduce both steering and support, since the employee is in the process of developing confidence and the ability to work independently. When the employee finally evolves to become an expert, the leader can delegate full responsibility to the employee to perform the assignments and assume they are performed well. This means that an expert has little need for specific guidance from the leader on how the job should be performed.

We have previously explained that the professions are based on an ideology where quality is top priority, and the professionals are mostly concerned with doing a good job. This means that professional workers have a number of characteristics with respect to motivation. When it comes to research on this topic, knowledge-based workers have been studied. Knowledge-based workers include both professionals and individuals with a large amount of knowledge based in a particular discipline (Newell et al., 2002). An example of the latter can be an economist or an information specialist. They have extensive knowledge in their fields, but are not necessarily formal members of any profession. Knowledge-based workers seem primarily motivated by the following four factors (Tampoe, 1993):

1. *Personal growth.* They are motivated by opportunities to realize their own potential.
2. *Autonomy.* They are motivated by work conditions that give them wide latitude with regard to performing the tasks they are responsible for.
3. *Goal achievement.* They are motivated by being able to achieve important quality-type goals of great significance for the organization.
4. *Fair reward.* They are motivated by fair wages that symbolize that they provide a valuable contribution to the organization's success.

Naturally, what motivates professionals is more complex than this. The individuals are different and are at various stages in their careers. Motivation must always be viewed in a developmental and situational perspective (Schein, 1988), and therefore there are no simple models for motivation. At the same time, it is important to note that professionals may have certain common characteristics. The reason for this may be that they all, out of personal motivations, have chosen a professional career, that they are part of a strong professional culture, or that they work in a particular job situation. Regarding leadership, it is therefore essential to reflect upon the distinctive qualities of the inner forces driving the employees.

A second point that has proven to be important in this context is how professionals think and reason – that is, the rationality or logic on which they base their decisions. Research has shown that there are indications of different rationalities in professional organizations (Fjellvær, 2010). Among others, bureaucratic, business, and professional rationalities have been identified.

Bureaucratic rationality is related to administration, and the emphasis is placed on systems, procedures, and structures. When confronted with the need to make a decision, it is rational to identify the formal rules and follow them. If there is a need to change the behaviour of the employees, the focus is often placed on the creation of new rules and procedures. This is a traditional form of rationality in the public sector, and it is important to ensure fairness, equality, and predictability in public administration.

Business rationality is more recent and has gained a foothold in the public sector over the last 30 years. As we mentioned in the Introduction, this prevalence may be linked to the international trend, namely "New Public Management," which represents the transfer of ways of thinking, methods, and techniques, from the private sector to the public sector. The core of this rationality is a goal-means approach. The main focus is on the results, and it is therefore rational to find the means that best fulfil the goals. Quite often, market-based solutions are seen as the most efficacious means. For example, users can choose freely between different public services (free choice of hospitals, free choice of primary-care physicians, free choice of school, etc.). Another example is when the private sector is given the opportunity to compete with the public sector in delivering public services.

A professional rationality operates on a different basis than both the bureaucratic and business rationality. This means that professional employees reason differently to other employees, although this difference is not absolute, as professionals also comply with formal rules and will search for methods that generate good results. However, their reasoning operates within the frameworks set by the profession's culture and the profession's identity. This means that decisions are justified by the fact that they are based on professional norms, values, and policies. This is a form of rationality that exists in all professions, despite the presence of variations based on the uniqueness of each profession. To sharpen these distinctions, we may set out the following:

Bureaucratic rationality:	Choose the activity that is consistent with a formal set of rules.
Business rationality:	Choose the activity that gives the best results.
Professional rationality:	Choose the activity that is consistent with professional values and professional standards.

These three ways of reasoning can create communication problems and conflicts in predominantly professional organizations. A professional employee has to relate to the requirement of following the formal rules, the requirement of finding cost-cutting measures, and the requirement of following professional standards. These requirements can often be in conflict with each other. A doctor, for example, may be forced to choose a costly treatment in order to care for a patient, and sometimes a doctor has to prioritize patients, which can lead to a violation of the formal waiting-list guarantee. In order to keep within a budget, a senior physician may be required to reduce the number of employees to a level that is unacceptable from a professional point of view.

Example 2

Rationalities in social work

One of the authors in his capacity as a senior manager in social work confronted these three rationalities. He needed to find a foster home for three children. Professionally, it was seen as a much better solution than an institution. A suitable foster family was available but they did not have enough room in their house. The usual municipality (bureaucratic) solution would be to provide a municipal house large enough. However, the foster family owned their house and did not wish to rent a house (or have one provided). A solution was proposed whereby the foster family would buy a larger house and the municipality would take part ownership in it which would be sold after the foster children no longer needed to be cared for. The need was for about eight years. However, in nice bureaucratic application of the rules, the project had to be costed over 20 years as it involved the purchase of property. The justification was not just professional and bureaucratic but also based on a straightforward business investment whereby the municipality would pay far less because they would be able to get back their ownership share in the property.

Because it is necessary to argue according to multiple rationalities, and not out of a need to follow the same rationality at all times, exercising leadership among professional employees requires managers to have insights into the dominant rationality within a profession. And value-based leadership requires leaders to have insights into the professional values. It is always a challenging task to become the leader of a predominantly professional organization without having a professional background. Communication becomes harder, and different rationalities lead to less understanding of how others think.

2.4   Summary

Professionalization has to be understood in the context of a range of literature. Some is focused upon the way in which a particular set of knowledge, skills or competences come to be identified as professional in nature. Professionalism is also about the creation of boundaries and the establishment of control over these boundaries. The characteristics of a profession have been explored in this chapter.

Freidson (2001) has offered some useful dimensions encompassing factors such as specialized expertise, control over a defined field, a protected labour market, a form of specialized higher education and an ideology focused on quality. Professionalism and education are closely related and this marks the development and demonstration of a progressive level of knowledge, skill, and competence.

Organizational factors and government regulation are also critical to the emergence and status of a profession. Mintzberg (1983) has identified a number of factors in professional organizations including a focus on service production, a high degree of decentralization and specialization, and formal requirements for worker qualifications.

Professional employees can also be seen in terms of stages of professional development ranging from beginner through stages of practice up to expert. Professions are often based upon knowledge work, and knowledge workers are typically motivated by factors such as personal growth, autonomy, goal achievement, and fair reward for their contribution.

Finally there are different rationalities – including bureaucratic, business, and professional ones – which are associated with different ways of reasoning leading to communication problems. Professionals and their management have to acknowledge and work with these differences.

Exercises for further development and understanding

- Do you consider yourself to be a professional? If so, then write down the factors which you would offer as evidence for this belief. If you do not consider yourself to be a professional, then what things would need to change in order for you to be able to so describe yourself?

- Can the government simply create a profession and control it without reference to the people who have been so determined? How would the writers of Professionalization theory regard such an attempt?

- Do professions have to share certain characteristics? Are there some factors which would be common to all professions? What professional aspects might an architect have in common with a nurse, for example?

- How might a profession be distinguished from a trade. Can the person who comes to repair your broken window, exercising a clear skill in the process, describe themselves as a professional?

Recommended further reading

Freidson, E. (2001). *Professionalism. The Third Logic.* Cambridge: Polity.
Newell, S., Robertson, M. Scarbrough, H. & Swan, J. (2002). *Managing Knowledge Work.* Basingstoke: Palgrave Macmillan.

Professional values and professional identity

3

Key learning points

At the end of this chapter the reader should be able to:

- understand the reasons for value development in the public sector
- be aware of the major values that are present in the public sector
- appreciate the key impact of professional values and identity for values-based leadership
- be aware of the importance of professional codes of conduct in shaping and determining values
- understand the ethical approaches which are especially pertinent to professional values
- understand how professional identity is constructed and maintained.

Professional employees are part of a complex universe of values. They are carriers of general social values, specific public values, specific organizational values, and values specific to their profession. Values of a profession are in a unique position and are largely linked to the duties within the profession. They serve as professional standards and provide guidelines for professional practice. Therefore, value-based leadership of professionals must to a large extent be based on the presence of a professional culture and a professional identity. This means that even though the leadership principles are the same, the value-based leadership exercised in practice varies from profession to profession. In this chapter we will first present the public universe of values. Thereafter we will examine the distinctive qualities of professional values, professional ethics, and professional identities.

3.1   The public universe of values

Today, the public sector is dominant in most societies, and includes a number of organizations and activities at national, regional, and local levels, which means that there is a wide diversity of values associated with the public sector. There have been many attempts at categorizing these values, although it has proven difficult to find a system which satisfies the requirements of making clear and consistent groupings (Rutgers, 2008). To give a picture of the public universe of values, we have chosen to start with a larger analysis of the research literature associated with the public sector, primarily within the leading journals in the United States, Great Britain, and the Scandinavian countries in the period 1990–2003 (Beck Jørgensen & Bozeman, 2007). The researchers identified a total of 72 values, and decided to organize them within seven different categories. Not all of these values are relevant for public professions, but they provide a solid overview of the universe of values which they are directly or indirectly a part of. The categories are as follows:

1.   Public sector's contribution to society
2.   Political organization (transfer of interests into decisions)
3.   The relation between public administration and politicians
4.   The relation between public administration and the environment
5.   Organizational aspects of public administration
6.   The behaviour of public-sector employees
7.   The relation between public administration and citizens

Public sector's contribution to society

Within this category, the researchers emphasize that the public sector should produce public goods. It should serve society as a whole and focus on all citizens of the society – that is, not to function as an extended arm for special interests. The researchers also emphasize altruism – that is, those working in the public sector should bear others in mind before themselves. They should be willing to bear another's burden and safeguard citizens' general and specific interests. These values are central to many public professions. Within this category, we also find the value of sustainability, meaning that a long-term perspective should be applied to the public sector's contributions. The interests of future generations should be taken into account when important decisions are made. The resources should not only be consumed, but they should also be managed for the benefit of both current and future generations. Finally, the public sector should not abuse its power but instead appear with dignity in the promotion of political stability. This is a broad category of values containing a relatively robust array of dimensions which capture the public sector's main function in society. Without these values, the basis for our way of organizing society might largely disappear.

Political organization (transfer of interests into decisions)

This category is linked to the political system. A large part of society's resources are transferred to the government through taxes, fees, etc. These resources are redistributed and attributed to a variety of interest groups in society. The system that allocates society's resources must have a high degree of legitimacy. Therefore, in this category, we primarily find values tied to democracy, with an emphasis on elections and decision making based on the majority in political bodies. In addition, we find values associated with different forms of user democracy in this category. These users might be represented in the governing bodies of public agencies, or might include citizens who are involved in political decisions in other ways.

The relation between public administration and politicians

The primary mission of employees in the public sector – especially in the administration – is to implement political decisions. Here, a central value in many countries is impartiality and political responsiveness. Politicians must be able to trust that the administration is able to adequately implement political decisions without being influenced by self-interest. Firstly, impartiality and political responsiveness includes responsibility – that is, public-sector employees must be accountable for their decisions regarding the implementation of policies. Secondly, it includes a form of responsiveness in relation to political processes. Since public-sector employees do not always work based on clear political decisions, they must to a large extent be able to interpret political signals and sometimes transfer policies into new applicable areas. Although these values are primarily related to public administration, they are also highly relevant for the leaders of public welfare production. Unit managers in school, health, and social services within a municipality are located relatively close to the politicians, and their organizational commitment to the chief administrative officer will indirectly include commitment to implement political decisions.

The relation between public administration and the environment

This category contains the values that capture employee responsibilities in relation to the surrounding community. These are values relevant to all employees in the public sector. Most importantly, this category contains values tied to transparency and discretion, which must be balanced against each other. On the one hand an open administration with a high degree of access rights is necessary if citizens – especially through the media – are to control the political and administrative processes. Many case documents are thus public and can be retrieved by anyone. In addition to this general right of access, many countries have also introduced a right for individuals to access the personal information that is stored about them. At the same time, we have values related to privacy and confidentiality. Personal information related to individuals should not be accessible to others without the individual's consent. There is also more general information that for different reasons is not made public.

Openness to the community also includes responsiveness in relation to public opinion. Employees in the public sector should keep up with what is happening in society so that, when necessary, they can adapt their work to new expectations from citizens. Although there are rules which set limitations on the activities of public enterprises, there is also room for discretion. This applies to both managers and employees. It is often possible to make adjustments which better account for society's needs. Yet what constitutes the "society's need" is a rather ambiguous concept. Obviously, public-sector employees will not meet the whole of society at large as this is an amorphous concept. Instead, they will typically meet individuals or groups that represent particular segments of society. Hence, the balancing of interests – typically competing ones – is another crucial value in this category. Which patients in a hospital should get first priority and which should be placed in a queue? Which students at a school should get access to additional support, and which must follow ordinary lessons? Which families should receive help from a children's welfare department? Which city district should get a new school? On a continual basis, politicians, public leaders, and employees must prioritize between possibly divergent interests. In order to prevent certain interest groups from exclusively setting the agenda, it is necessary to achieve an adequate balance between legitimate but competing interests.

In short, the relation between public-sector employees and the environment to a large extent represents a balance between openness and discretion and a balance between the interests of different groups. It is here that both managers and employees confront a variety of dilemmas during the normal workday.

Organizational aspects of public administration

This category includes values related to creating a well-functioning organization, and consists of three main value groups. The first group captures the values that over time affect the organization's resilience, which is in part a function of stability and adaptability. A robust public organization must be stable so that it is sufficiently predictable. This is ensured by a more bureaucratic form of organization in which the behaviour of employees is largely governed by rules. The need for stability can also be provided through a strong professional culture and social control – which is common in all markedly professional organizations. At the same time, there is a need for adaptability in the sense that bureaucracy and professional culture must not be so strong that the organization fails to adapt to new conditions. Alongside stability and adaptability, another value related to resilience is reliability in implementing political decisions, addressing assigned tasks, and serving the needs of interest groups. The second group of values is tied to the ability to innovate, which is an extension of being adaptable. Innovation captures the importance of finding completely new solutions as a way of meeting a dynamic society. A school must be able to implement new pedagogical principles as a way to meet the challenges posed by social media, for example. Likewise, the police need to develop new investigative methods as a way to take advantage of new technologies. Perhaps an organization itself needs to change to improve functionality.

The last group of values contains ones related to the efficient use of available resources. Resources in the public sector are always scarce, and it is therefore necessary to husband them. The core value in this group is good productivity – that is, high production in relation to resource consumption. These values are also found in various forms of management control, often focused on cost control and production volume.

The behaviour of public-sector employees

This category is aimed directly at the individual employee and captures the values which are believed to regulate behaviour at work. Here we find the individual values of professionalism, honesty, moral, ethical awareness, and integrity. The first value represents the many dimensions related to professional occupations. Indeed, professionalism is a composite value where the contents to a certain extent vary between professions even though there is always a common core. The other values are more general, pointing out some personal qualities that are desirable for the employees in the public sector to hold. All the values are important, and we often find them encapsulated in formal ethical rules. If we were to highlight one single value as important, it would perhaps be integrity. People with high integrity naturally possess many of the other values and represent these in different situations. This is reflected in surveys where citizens indicate that they place higher trust in certain occupational categories that others.

The relation between public administration and citizens

This is a comprehensive category that captures the central values of the relationship between the citizen and the public sector. There are four main groups: legality, sense of justice, dialogue, and user orientation. The values related to legality capture many of the values inherent in our formal legal system, including individual rights and equal treatment, but also the rule of law and justice. This is a stable group of values, each of which is thoroughly integrated with the other values, and each is regulated by law.

Values in the second group are connected to a sense of justice, and complement the first group by emphasizing fairness and professionalism. The laws should be interpreted and applied with some degree of discretion, and one should not just look at the words in the law but also at its intentions. This is important in all law-based societies.

The third group emphasizes dialogue and captures the values of responsiveness, user democracy, citizen participation, and citizen opportunities for self-development. In other words, the focus is on the citizens' direct contact with the public sector, with emphasis on employees being able to identify needs, wishes, criticism, and other forms of feedback. Opportunities for citizen self-development should also be emphasized. All in all, the third group should consist of a dialogue where both parties have the opportunity for learning.

Finally, the values associated with user orientation will focus on the relations between individual employees and the users. Here we find values like kindness, respect, and orderliness. Users should feel that they are taken seriously, are being listened to, and are treated appropriately.

As we see, there are many values that can be linked to the public sector. And even if the values are organized into separate categories, there is a certain overlap – some values can be placed in multiple categories. The public universe of values is both diverse and complex, and it may be beneficial to look for some core values. Are there any values which are more important than others and that are also valid for the entire public sector?

The concept of the public-sector ethos is used to capture such values, where a rough distinction can be made between democratic values and economic values (Lundquist, 1998). Within each of these groups are individual values that mutually support each other. Democratic values consist of political democracy, rule of law, and public ethics, while the economic values consist of goal–means rationality, productivity, and cost effectiveness. While democratic values are specific to the public sector and contribute to the sector's own identity, economic values are present in both public and private enterprises. The public ethos is in this context represented by democratic values (Lundquist, 1998).

A thorough analysis of the values present in the public sector in Denmark has been conducted in an effort to find a more precise definition of the public ethos (Beck-Jørgensen, 2003b), where researchers looked for values that were both central to all administrative levels and to various welfare-producing organizations. They concluded that a core of public values exist and consist of basic ones, including general social responsibility, public insight, the rule of law, independent professional standards, efficiency, and equality. These values were represented in a broad range of public organizations and were therefore described as a general public ethos.

They also concluded that these core values were a key part of a common public identity. The researchers identified a layer of what is referred to as a field-specific ethos outside this core – an ethos tied to a specific education and often a specific professional area. These values are part of the professional culture and will vary according to which professions are represented in the organization. This layer was also considered relatively stable. The next layer was associated with a leadership and workplace ethos, which includes values related to leadership, management, and human resources of each organization. These values are in other words values that underlie organizational culture, and thus they will vary from organization to organization. These studies show that professionals must adhere to some general public values, the prevailing organizational cul-ture, and their own professional culture. In practice, of course, some values are more relevant than others. A teacher at a school, a nurse at a hospital, or a lawyer in the state administration are all public officers, yet they will encounter different values in their typical workday. In value-based leadership, it is therefore important to be able to sort out the most important values. The focus should be set on the values which, in a given situation, are of greatest importance for the work to be performed.

In the context of value-based leadership, it can be interesting to consider where values are placed in public leadership platforms. Even though it is a prob-lem that leadership platforms to some degree are aimed at providing a better reputation and legitimacy, they at the same time represent values which are considered especially important for the society.

In the UK, after a series of scandals relating to public officials in the 1990s, a committee to examine standards in public life was established. The report led to the adoption of what came to be known as the Nolan Values which are widely regarded as the basis for behaviour by both elected politicians and public officials. They have also been generally accepted by third-sector organizations as having general applicability for organizations and people who hold positions of public trust or who are operating in the context of public funding. These are shown in Example 3. The principles so indicated are arguably a basis for public and elected officials in all countries which ac-knowledge the importance of democratic process and fairness and impartiality in public office

Example 3

The Nolan values of public life

Selflessness
Holders of public office should act solely in terms of the public interest. They should not do so in order to gain financial or other benefits for themselves, their family, or their friends.

Integrity
Holders of public office should not place themselves under any financial or other obligation to outside individuals or organizations that might seek to influ-ence them in the performance of their official duties.

Objectivity
In carrying out public business, including making public appointments, award-ing contracts, or recommending individuals for rewards and benefits, holders of public office should make choices on merit.

Accountability
Holders of public office are accountable for their decisions and actions to the public, and must submit themselves to whatever scrutiny is appropriate to their office.

Openness
Holders of public office should be as open as possible about all the decisions and actions that they take. They should give reasons for their decisions and restrict information only when the wider public interest clearly demands it.

Honesty
Holders of public office have a duty to declare any private interests relating to their public duties and to take steps to resolve any conflicts arising in a way that protects the public interest.

Leadership
Holders of public office should promote and support these principles by leadership and example.

Today it is more and more common to develop both overarching and business-specific lists of core values for public leadership (Kernaghan, 2003; Pollach, 2005; Wæraas, 2010). In Norway, the government published "Platform for leadership in the state," which served up some key principles that should form the basis for all government leaders. This document clarifies that leadership in the state should be distinctly anchored in values, some of which are explicit while others are formulated in more indirect ways. It is initially stated that leadership should be based on fundamental values with strong roots in Norwegian culture and traditions. Reference is also made that many of these values are universal and are expressed through a series of human rights conventions to which Norway is bound. The two most important value categories presented in this document are as follows:

1. democratic values (representative government, freedom of speech, equality, participation, empowerment, community responsibility, user orientation, and transparency)
2. values in a rule-of-law-state (legality, neutrality, equal treatment, justice, predictability, and contradiction – the latter entails the possibility of defending oneself when faced with a legal case).

This demonstrates that leadership at the uppermost level of the Norwegian state is constituted by values consistent with democracy and the rule of law. Although less direct perhaps, there are several other values conveyed in the leadership platform. The most important are:

- efficiency (results-oriented, resource utilization, user orientation)
- empowerment (participation, trust, transparency, collaborative culture)
- collaboration (internal and external)
- learning and development (skills, learning environment, work environment, diversity)
- loyalty (on political decisions and to the public).

All these values are given weight. We note the relatively small emphasis placed on ethical values, values related to the individual employee's behaviour, and values related to various professions. These values are regulated by a set of ethical rules that were later approved by the Norwegian authorities. These rules are connected to general provisions, loyalty, transparency, trust in public administration, and professional independence and objectivity. Altogether, the leadership platform and the ethical rules of conduct create a strong value basis for the Norwegian public sector.

3.2   Professional values

We regard the research basis for an overarching theory of professional culture as not well developed. Part of the reason for this is that research into the topic is constrained by the boundaries of professions. In other words, we have research related to the teaching profession, the medical profession, the nursing profession, etc., rather than research that cuts across professions. In order to acquire insight into professional values, it can be prudent to begin by exploring theories of organizational culture – especially those from the functional perspective. These can provide a theoretical framework that cuts across professional boundaries, but at the same time interfaces with values that are more specific to each profession.

Organizational culture can be seen as resulting from a long-term process whereby norms and values emerge in response to the need to adapt to the environment and the necessity of creating a well-integrated organization. From this perspective, organizational culture is not something that can simply be used as a tool to achieve goals. The culture is a response to the past and present challenges facing the organization and is relatively stable over time. Since the organizational entities can face various challenges when interacting with the environment, it is natural that subcultures within the organization emerge.

One of the leading representatives of this perspective is Edgar Schein (1988). He sees the organizational culture as an integration mechanism that creates a sense of belonging and community spirit that makes it easier to adapt to the environment. Culture is not a variable that can be confined – it is an integrated part of the entire organization. Schein defines organizational culture as follows:

> Organizational culture represents a pattern of shared basic assumptions learned by a group as it solved its problems of external adaptation and internal integration, which has worked well enough to be considered valid and, therefore to be taught to new members as the correct way to perceive, think and feel in relation to those problems. (Schein, 2010, p. 18)

Organizational culture contributes in other words to creating a common understanding of the external reality and a common way of relating to this. Thus, organizational culture becomes an occipital model of behaviour or action. Or put another way, organizational culture is rather like a programme that controls the behaviour of the organizational members. They key elements of organizational culture entail a common understanding of reality and common values.

According to Schein, organizational culture has two main functions, namely external adaptation and internal integration. The former affects the organization's connection with the environment, while the latter contributes to the organization's internal integration. With respect to the external function, emphasis is placed on the organization's development of socially acceptable goals and methods. Simply put, organizational culture must conform with expectations in the environment. With respect to the internal function, the aim is to create a well-functioning and thoroughly integrated organization, which requires several conditions: a common "language" and conceptual framework, common rules governing the relationship between the organization's members, a common understanding of what is right and wrong, and a common understanding of reality. Organizational culture is a kind of invisible glue that binds the organization's parts together and creates unity and internal coherence. Based on this, we can argue that a profession's culture has two main functions: (a) an external function to ensure the profession's legitimacy and acceptance in its surroundings; and (b) an internal function which contributes to internal integration.

In the professions the external function is maintained by a professional umbrella structure, under which we find both national and international professional organizations. Within nursing, for example, most countries have large national nursing associations. And at the international level, we find "The International Council of Nurses" (ICN), which has developed an international code of ethics for nurses. Similar organizations are found in many public professions, extending across national borders and working actively with their own values, thus ensuring the professional culture operates as a tool for maintaining and developing the profession's legitimacy.

The external function of a profession's culture is also maintained at a lower level. When representatives from various professions interact in their local environments, their value bases often appear and contribute to more localized forms of legitimacy. In a municipality, for example, local members of a relevant profession might be asked to comment on a particular media case. Perhaps local teachers or their organizations are asked to comment on the problems of bullying in schools, or maybe a local social worker is asked to say something about the quality of home nursing-care or social welfare. When a professional makes a statement on behalf of the profession, he or she often directly or indirectly bases their statements on the standards and ethical guidelines within their profession. Thus, the professional culture contributes to what we call external adaptation.

The internal function of a profession's culture is primarily addressed at the organizational level. While organizational culture creates a community within the organization, the profession's culture helps with collaboration between professionals. It provides common terminology, decides who can be a member, defines the power and status of the members, forms the basis for close relationships, regulates rewards and punishments, and provides an ideological basis for membership.

So, what forms the basis for the profession's values? One of the characteristics of a profession is its foundations on an ideology that promotes greater motivation to do a good job rather than to achieve economic benefits; that is, there is a greater focus on quality than on efficiency (Freidson, 2001). Put simply, the content of the job is the focus. This will also affect the basis for values, and we can generally say that values are related to the:

- *specific objectives* to be realized by a profession (terminal values)
- *professional standards* that govern behaviour within the profession (instrumental values).

These two suggest that each profession has its own specific set of values, especially with regard to instrumental ones. At the same time, there is greater overlap in the terminal values of organizations. Some of these have a general character, such as putting students, clients, or users "at the centre." Therefore, the cultures of the various professions in the public sector have many overlapping areas. If we compare the values of social workers and preschool teachers, we will find that they both heavily stress the relationship with users. Both disadvantaged families and kindergarten children are to be taken care of and offered good quality service. However, when looking at instrumental values – that is, the professional standards in use – there are large differences between the two professions, where the tasks of a social worker are based on different methods than those of a preschool teacher.

To demonstrate this, we can take a closer look at some professions which are heavily represented in the public sector, starting with nursing. The American Association of Colleges of Nursing (AACN) has formulated five core values of this profession (Shaw & Degazon, 2008):

1. *Altruism.* The interests of others are set higher than self-interests, meaning that nurses will work to meet their patients' needs without having to think about how this influences their own rewards.

2. *Autonomy.* Nurses should have wide latitude in the job so they can leverage their expertise and use their professional judgement to the benefit of their patients.
3. *Human dignity.* Nurses should have respect for the human values related to patients, their families, and society as a whole, and this should be the basis for all communication with these groups.
4. *Integrity.* The work carried out by nurses is in accordance with the profession's ethical codes and accepted professional standards.
5. *Social justice.* Nurses shall conduct their work in accordance with moral, legal, and humanistic principles. This value provides a basis for decisions related to an equitable distribution of health services and the allocation of resources to education and to the maintenance of a good work environment.

This shows that the nursing profession has a broad value base and encompasses several fundamental elements. *Altruism* shows that the patient is at the centre, which is a value that captures a number of more detailed values on how patients should be treated. As shown by *autonomy*, the nurses' tasks and professional latitude are also important, where professional knowledge and utilization of knowledge are key. At the same time, we see that *integrity* also provides a framework for how knowledge is utilized: It should be carried out within accepted professional standards and ethical codes. These two values – autonomy and integrity – show the strong emphasis on professional practice being governed by both individual employees and the profession. On a slightly different note, *human dignity* creates a link between professional values and key values in society, while the value *social justice* creates a link to what we have defined as public values. These two values act as bridges between the profession and its surroundings.

To demonstrate the breadth of the professions' core values, we will take a closer look at the US Marine Corps. It specifies three key values (http://www.marines.com/history-heritage/principles-values):

Example 4

Values in the US Marines

Honour
"A code of personal integrity, honor guides those who do the right thing when no one is looking. It is not only a duty, but also a distinction, as those who possess honor are held in honor. It's found in one's beliefs, but exhibited through one's actions. Marines are held to the highest of standards, ethically and morally. Marines are expected to act responsibly in a manner befitting the title they've earned."

Courage
"When other principles are tested, it's courage that prevents them from crumbling. It isn't ignoring fear, but being stronger than fear. Courage is the

guardian of all other values. It is there when times are toughest, when difficult decisions have to be made. It takes the form of mental, physical and ethical strength, and is found in the backbone of every Marine."

Commitment
"Commitment is the spirit of determination found in every Marine. It is what compels Marines to serve our nation and the Corps, and to continue on when others quit. Commitment doesn't take breaks and it cannot be faked. It measures and proves one's desire, dedication and faithfulness. Becoming a United States Marine represents the highest level of commitment."

As we can see, there are many dimensions within each of these values that complement the value base. We see that the values largely reflect the task that a profession is responsible for.

To what extent are such value platforms reflected in practice? Research has shown that within the nursing profession, the values that concern the relationship between themselves and patients are given the highest priority (Rassin, 2008). Altruism was only ranked twelfth, and values related to responsibility to their own profession and to the community were given low priority. This indicates that for nurses, contact with the patients is the most important. There may therefore be a difference between the formal set of values created for a profession and the professional values that are present in its everyday practice.

3.3   Professional codes of conduct

Within each profession there is a stronger focus on professional ethics than on professional values. It can, however, be debated whether or not it is possible to make a conceptual distinction between professional values and professional ethics. Professional codes of ethics have a clear value base and appear frequently as an operationalization of values. In other words, they are specified so that they can provide guidance for practical professional conduct.

In principle, professional values are a broader concept than professional ethics. Within ethical theory we can distinguish between several main directions. However, we will here concentrate on the following three ethical theories:

1. Virtue ethics
2. Deontological ethics
3. Proximity ethics.

Virtue ethics is related to Aristotle (384–322 BC), who focused on what constitutes a good life for humans. This form of ethics is aimed at developing the positive aspects of the human being – honesty, helpfulness, caring, courage, etc. In other words, the actor is in focus, not the actions. It is the person's ethical character that is essential for the action's ethical value. With such a starting point, it becomes important to develop people with an ethical character. Therefore, a code of conduct based on virtue ethics sets the professional practitioner at the centre.

The second direction of ethics is related to Kant (1724–1804), who shifted the focus from the good to the appropriate behaviour. This form of ethics is often called *deontological ethics*, and it focuses on what are the appropriate actions. To narrow it down, we can say that the requirement for an ethical action is that it should be able to function as a norm for the desirable behaviour in a society. The action should therefore be within the relevant instrumental values. There is a duty to perform the correct action without any reflection on the action's impact. While virtue ethics is aimed at the individual's characteristics, deontological ethics is aimed at human action.

Within the healthcare and social professions, *proximity ethics* has also played a central role. Although it can be considered as an alternative to deontological ethics, the two forms of ethics can also complement each other. Proximity ethics is particularly associated with Knud Løgstrup (1905–81), whose book on the subject entitled *The Ethical Demand* was published in 1956. Here, the focus is set on the ethical dimension that occurs in social contexts – in the interaction between people. The question is, then, what personal characteristics can help to develop good social relationships. This is a universal question relevant in all cultures where people meet. Løgstrup uses the concept of *the ethical demand* to indicate that a demand for ethical behaviour arises when human beings interact. We are confronted with a universal and social responsibility to act ethically in interactions with other people. Trust is in this context a key variable. Trust between people is a fundamental prerequisite for the development of ethical relationships. And trust comes before mistrust. Trust in other people is woven into the human condition. Mistrust arises because of a betrayal of the ethical demand. Levinas (1906–95) uses the metaphor of *the other's face* to convey a similar form of ethics. The other's face and the other's glance will create a sense of responsibility and obligation to ethical awareness and ethical action. When the individual recognizes himself in the other, a relation will emerge between the humans who are otherwise far apart. This is particularly relevant in relations between people of different social status, power, and influence. The ethical responsibility is as strongly present in meeting with people who operate outside the usual norms of society.

These three forms of ethics are illustrated in Figure 3.1, which shows that virtue ethics, deontological ethics, and proximity ethics are in many ways linked together. Although they are independent theories, they often capture some of the same dilemmas. As such, they all provide valuable insights into the profession's ethical challenges.

There are other theories of ethics; the most relevant here is *the ethics of consequences (Consequentialism)*. The basic thought is that the appropriate action

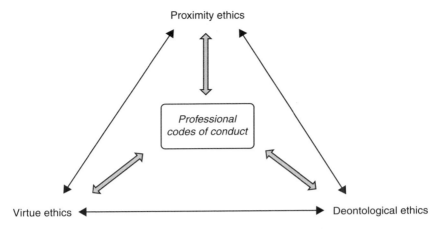

Proximity ethics

Professional
codes of conduct

Virtue ethics   Deontological ethics

Figure 3.1   Various types of ethical approaches

can only be assessed on the basis of the consequence of the action. For example, a user of public services wants to give one of the public employees a gift in appreciation of good treatment. Based on the deontological ethics, there may be a rule against receiving donations from the users, and the employee must thus politely refuse the gift. By contrast, the ethics of consequences necessitates an examination of the situation. If the gift leads to a debt of gratitude that can provide the donor with future benefits, it is ethically correct to decline the gift. However, if there is no such adverse consequence, it is not unethical to receive the gift. Based on virtue ethics, the professionals make the right action in line with their good personal qualities.

Within ethics of professions, the focus has been on virtue ethics and deontological ethics. If we bring these two theories into the field of professional ethics, the question is whether we should focus on developing a good professional worker who represents the central virtues, or whether we will develop a set of rules which ensure that professional employees behave in an ethical manner. Within the teaching profession, this has created a debate that contributed to the profession deciding not to prepare an overarching ethical framework (Colnerud, 2006). The argument against establishing a set of ethical rules is that it does not necessarily contribute to the development of better ethical practices. Instead, it may create a dependence on rules that prevents ethical reflection. We get a set of rules that deprive employees of the ethical responsibility for their own practices. They become more concerned with following the rules than reflecting on whether they comply with the overall values of the profession.

There are many within the teaching profession who argue that the focus should instead be placed on virtue ethics; that is, the development of a practical wisdom associated with moral virtues. In the literature that discuss whether ethical codes should be developed for the teaching profession, the positions span from full support to complete rejection, even though most people realize that the moral and ethical responsibilities of teachers are far greater than what can be specified in a set of ethical rules (Campbell, 2008). The question is whether or not we can answer "Yes, thank you – I'll have both" (Nyeng, 2002). Is it possible to develop a set of general rules that can form a basis for ethical reflection? Could this reflection contribute to a process in which teachers' virtues come into focus (Colnerud, 2006)? This means that a foundation based on a synthesis between a virtue ethics and deontological ethics can create a fruitful dialogue within the profession.

Another important aspect of the teaching profession is that it has some characteristics that distinguish it from other professions. The relationship between teacher and student has a different character to that between a nurse and a patient or between a lawyer and a client. While mutual confidence is fundamental in most professions, this has a different nature in a teacher–student relationship. It is less essential for the student to understand the rationale behind a teacher's actions, and the teacher is in a position of power that is unique when compared to other professional workers. It is also important that teachers appear as role models for students and that this be an integral part of the teaching profession (Carr, 2005). Based on this, it can be hard to differentiate between teachers' personal and professional values, which can be tied to virtue and duty, respectively. In other words, the duty-related dimension is tied to professional ethical codes, while the virtue-related dimension is linked to the characteristics of teachers as human beings.

The question of which ethical theories should be applied has created a dilemma within several professions. This has contributed to the ethical guidelines changing over time. As an example of this, we can look at the professional ethical guidelines for Norwegian social workers (Eide, 2008). The first ethical guidelines were prepared in 1967 and had a clear deontological orientation. The focus was on what social workers should do, and the guidelines were completely independent of context, meaning that they were general and not tied to specific situations or challenges that the social workers might meet in their work. These guidelines were replaced in 1989 by a *Statement of ethical principles in social work*. Although the overall content was much of the same, this amendment represented a transition from specific rules to more general values. Thus, interpretation and reflection would be needed to a greater extent. Although the values were still independent of context, a reflection on values would lead to a stronger connection between values and practice. The social worker also appeared more as an ethical actor, which created a link to virtue ethics. The principles of 1989 were continued in 2002 through a new set of rules for professional ethics. Here the principles were maintained and adjusted and now contained both a value basis and a set of ethical rules aimed at regulating the relationship between the practitioner and his immediate environment. A particular emphasis was placed on the relation between practitioner and client/user, which indicates that proximity ethics has also been important when designing the new rules.

The latter document is aimed at child welfare officers, social workers, and social educators. It is a great example of the design of professional ethical guidelines, and after an introduction it contains the following key points:

Example 5

Statement of ethical principles at work from the Norwegian Union of Social Educators and Social Workers

Fundamental values

Presented here are the profession's core values. First, reference is made to the various UN conventions on human rights and international ethical guidelines for health and social work. Then, a set of principles which are to be applicable to the respective professions is presented. These principles represent the specific base values, as defined in the following:

- Human life is inviolable
- Respect for the individual
- A holistic view of humans
- Equality and non-discrimination
- Trust, openness, honesty, care, and compassion
- Confidentiality and professional secrecy
- Responsibility to alert and notify
- Justice
- Solidarity
- Equality before the law
- Individual responsibility.

The relation between the practitioner and the user/client

In this section a number of guidelines were set up to regulate the relationship between the professional practitioner and the clients. The guidelines were formulated at a relatively general level and can therefore invite reflection on how to interpret and apply them in practice. The guidelines include the following points:

- the meeting between individuals
- loyalty
- empowerment
- authority and power
- enforcement
- discretion and power of judgement
- duty of confidentiality.

Under these points, various dilemmas that professionals may encounter in their practice are presented. This way, they also offer more specific guidelines for ethical reflection.

Relation to colleagues, employers, and society
In this section, the ethical guidelines on the following conditions are formulated:
- co-operation
- loyalty
- notification responsibilities.

If we perform a detailed analysis of this professional ethics document, we will see that there is an overlap between the postulated values and the more specific ethical guidelines. The guidelines are therefore largely an elaboration of the value base. Although the ethical basis provides good opportunities for ethical reflection, it is still primarily a deontological design insofar as the focus is placed on the practitioner's professional actions. Still, an approach that comes closer to virtue ethics may be applied when reflecting on these principles.

If we compare this document with other guidelines for professional ethics, we will find both similarities and differences. For starters, while the document here contains an ethical value base that is explicitly applied, the international code of ethics for nurses (The ICN Code of Ethics for Nurses, 2006), for example, lacks such an explicit value base. This absence is also found in a variety of other international codes of ethics for professional occupations. Moreover, the document here acts as a more robust starting point for ethical reflection, whereas the ethical basis for nurses contains, for example, explicit ethical rules.

The similarity in the documents is that the ethical rules are tied to the relationship between the professional practitioner and the immediate stakeholders – in this case the user/client, colleagues, employers, and society. After a review of the ethical codes for education (Öztürk, 2010), the conclusion is that these documents are often organized around four categories:

1. Commitment to children
2. Commitment to parents and family
3. Commitment to community
4. Commitment to the profession.

There are different codes of ethics within each of these categories, which to some extent are adapted to the context in which they operate. The same division is found within a variety of health professions, where the focus is on the relationship between the professional practitioner and her surroundings.

Therefore, codes of ethics in professional occupations have many similarities, although all professions seem to find their own variations as well. They constitute clear illustrations of what a desired professional culture looks like. The word "desired" is used to signify that the real professional culture is often different from the picture given by codes (Hunt, 2004). Real culture is created from close interactions between professional workers, where different elements character- ize the culture that is created in practice. The codes of ethics are important in this process, although they can be interpreted in different ways. And even though some principles are more present than others, the codes contribute to a foundation for ethical reflection and ethical practices.

3.4   Professional identity

Professional identity has a weaker theoretical basis than organizational identity. At the same time, the theoretical foundations for both of these concepts are anchored in social identity theory. It is therefore possible to analyse professional identity out from the insights developed through research on organizational identity.

Most theories in this area explicitly or implicitly make the assumption that organizational identity is a cognitive concept that has behavioural consequences (Ravasi & van Rekom, 2003); that is, experienced identity affects the judg- ments, decisions, and actions of its members. This means that it has a content that can be described and identified by the individual person. In a definition of the concept, focus is placed on three dimensions (Albert & Whetten, 1985):

1. Organizational identity should be seen as a central character of the organiza- tion – the criterion of claimed central character.
2. It should distinguish the organization from other organizations – the crite- rion of claimed distinctiveness.
3. It should over time represent a certain degree of continuity/stability – the criterion of claimed temporal continuity.

The first dimension indicates that organizational identity must be based on as- pects that have some significance. Most organizations have a host of character- istics. All hospitals have doctors and nurses, an emergency room, and a director. The core question is which of these characteristics are important enough to be an essential part of the organization's identity. More important characteristics are that a hospital is publicly owned, that altruism is a core value, and that hy- giene is an important instrumental value.

The second dimension indicates that organizational identity should distin- guish the organization from other organizations. In other words, it should cap- ture dimensions that highlight inter-organizational differences, thus making it meaningful to talk about us and them. For example, hospitals will have an iden- tity that distinguishes them from schools, social service offices, kindergartens, and other public welfare services. At the same time, an organizational identity will pinpoint other organizations which have elements similar to one's own.

Finally, the definition of these characteristics must have certain stability over time. They must have persisted for some years and should be relatively unaffected by short-term changes in society. Organizational characteristics that can change quickly due to political decisions will not be very suitable as part of an organizational identity.

Research has documented a strong correlation between organizational culture and organizational identity (Hatch & Schultz, 2002). The value base is of great importance for "who we are," and will over time become an important part of identity. Meanwhile, organizational identity will also influence the organization's culture because identity is, as previously mentioned, a cognitive concept, which means we can talk about it and give it concrete contents. And the values which we talk about will over time build up in the culture.

This means that professional identity has a clear connection to the culture of a profession. Because of this, both the formal value base in the profession's code of ethics and the actual values that are developed within the professional community will be depicted in the profession's identity. Therefore, professional identity is highly important in developing value-based leadership, especially since identity to a greater extent than culture is a cognitive concept.

We have earlier in this chapter stated that the core values of the US Marine Corps are honour, courage, and commitment. An example of their identity is captured by the concept of "semper fidelis" (http://www.marines.com/history-heritage/principles-values):

Example 6

Semper Fidelis in the US Marines

"Semper Fidelis distinguishes the Marine Corps bond from any other. It goes beyond teamwork – it is a brotherhood that can be counted on. Latin for "always faithful," Semper Fidelis became the Marine Corps motto in 1883. It guides Marines to remain faithful to the mission at hand, to each other, to the Corps and to the country, no matter what. Becoming a Marine is a transformation that cannot be undone, and Semper Fidelis is a permanent reminder of that. Once made, a Marine will forever live by the ethics and values of the Corps. In addition to Semper Fidelis, Marine Corps Officers also embrace the phrase Ductos Exemplo, "to lead by example," the motto of Officer Candidates School (OCS). Instructors look for candidates who display self-reliance, discipline and responsibility. Desire and motivation to lead Marines are deciding factors in an officer´s success."

While organizational identity is linked to the "we" and thus captures group identity, professional identity is linked to the "I," allowing us to argue that theories of professional identity to a large extent stress the development of the individual practitioner's identity. What does it mean for the individual employee to be a teacher, doctor, nurse, soldier, police officer, or a member of another professional group? This has led to a larger concern about identity development in the various professions rather than professional identity as a concept. Therefore, there is a lot of knowledge about how a professional career influences a profession's identity, but less knowledge of what lies behind the concept of professional identity. It is also challenging for the general concept that much of the knowledge which has been developed is profession-specific. The research is aimed at a specific vocation, and there is little discussion of whether the insights developed are transferable to other professions.

On a general level, we can start off with identity theory, which has been developed for knowledge-based workers (Wenger, 1998). It links the identity to what is called a community of practice. This is a group of individuals whose bonds aim at developing knowledge and competence of a specific domain. For starters, a community of practice is characterized by a shared involvement and a shared commitment to learning. Moreover, members have a common goal and a common vision, and they feel responsible for realizing this vision. Ultimately, the members have a common repertoire of methods and instruments for, among other things, solving specific tasks, or they may have a common understanding about how "things are connected." While this is a fairly loose definition, the key point is that members meet and form a functional learning community. A group of professional employees who meet at or outside of work will satisfy these conditions. They are engaged in their profession, they have a common vision of what their contributions to society will be, and they have common professional standards, a shared value base, and often a common picture of their own identity.

An identity highly connected to practice will develop within a community of practice. This identity will in other words be characterized by the experience created in daily work. As specified by Wenger (1998), identity in this context will be characterized as:

1. Complex and experience-based
2. Not fixed but constantly evolving
3. Having a strong social character
4. Forming a timeline between past, present, and future
5. Integrating the experiences of various practice communities
6. Created in the interface between the local and the global.

Let us look a little closer at the possible consequences for professional workers. First of all, the professional identity is created through *practical experience*. This means, for example, that the identity of a doctor is created through experience in the job. In other words, the medical identity evolves in the consultations with patients. The question "Who am I as a professional practitioner?" is therefore related to the individual's work experience. The second point shows that professional identity is more of a *process* than a state. A doctor's identity is therefore to some extent always in motion as the identity is created and re-created continuously.

Furthermore, professional identity has a strong *social* character. It is created in social contexts within the communities of practice. Our experience-based identity will be confirmed and developed in conjunction with other people. The teacher's identity is created in the classroom, in joint meetings, and in all social contexts where teachers meet. "Who I am" is merging with "who we are." Professional identity is therefore a strong common identity.

Point No. 4 indicates that the question "Who am I today?" is inextricably linked with both past experiences and expectations about the future. It is like a *timeline* giving meaning to the past and expectations about the future. We can say that identity development is a learning process that places things in context.

The fifth point indicates that if a professional worker has a variety of experiences, the professional identity appears as an *integrated whole* of the total experience. In the course of a career, many professionals will be in communities of practice in various forms. The first communities of practice often occurs during training, where students get together to reflect on their experiences from practice. Later, the career path can lead to work at various administrative levels, in different positions, and in different institutions. This causes the individual to enter various communities of practice. Professional identity will then bridge these experiences and contribute to an integrated experience of oneself as a professional practitioner.

The final point indicates that the identity has both a *local and global character*. Although an identity is created locally, it will be in a global perspective. Professional identity created in practice will therefore be enhanced and developed through participation in a national and international community. A social worker who conducts his/her work in a small Norwegian municipality will thus identify himself with social workers in all parts of the world.

We see that the theory of knowledge management gives us a nuanced and overall picture of what the concept of professional identity entails. For a more detailed picture of professional identity, we must turn to the theory developed for each profession. Although these theories have a strong connection to a particular profession, much of the knowledge is relevant for other professions. We find, for example, a great deal of research on professional identity within the teaching profession. A major review of the research in this area (Beijaard et al., 2004) concludes that there is little common understanding of what lies in this concept. In summary, four issues are highlighted as potentially important in understanding teachers' professional identity:

1. Professional identity is an ongoing process of interpreting and re-interpreting experiences. This means that the development of identity is considered a lifelong learning process. And it will combine both "who I am today" and "who I will be tomorrow."
2. Professional identity includes both person and context. Although teachers have a shared value base and professional backgrounds, they will interpret and handle these in a personal way. There is therefore always a difference between the "I-identity" and the "we-identity." Everybody is a self-standing individual even while being part of the same community.

3. The professional identity is made up of sub-identities that are more or less in harmony with each other. Some of these can be well integrated and form a strong core within the overarching identity. Other sub-identities may have a weaker link to the overarching one. The tighter the interconnectedness between sub-identities, the harder it is to change or remove any one of them.
4. The professional identity is influenced by individuals' self-interest. The professionals will deliberately try to develop their own identity in the desired direction.

We see from these points that there is a relatively large similarity between the research related to the teaching profession and the general description of what characterizes the identity of knowledge-based workers (Wenger, 1998).

Research has shown that professional identity is developed over a relatively long time. Identity is created through a complex process in which professional practitioners obtain an image of both their discipline and their role as professional practitioners. Professional socialization can in this context be defined as a process where a professional acquires the skills, knowledge, values, and attitudes which belong to the group they want to join (Merton, 1968). It is demonstrated that within the teaching profession, new teachers go through different phases in their identity development (see Flores & Day, 2006 for a review). The first phase consists of a threshold that must be overcome. This may happen during the practice or during the first full-time teaching position. It is described as a "transition shock" (Veenman, 1984) and can be viewed as a battle where the teachers on the one hand are trying to adapt their practice to their own visions of being a teacher, and on the other hand are trying to adapt to the requirement of being socialized into the school culture (Day, 1999). Through their education, student teachers have developed an image of what it means to be a teacher, how the teaching profession should be handled, and what values are most central to the profession. Professional identity is created in a process where the image must be adapted to the realities facing the students when entering the profession. During this process, the teachers' personal qualifications, their past experiences, the school culture, and the school leadership are of importance.

Research in the health professions shows some of the same development patterns. It is described as an attempt to balance between the values that form the basis of education and those present in healthcare organizations (Mooney, 2007). Within the nursing profession, older and experienced nurses are especially important for the development of identity among newly hired nurses (Henderson, 2002). The tacit and implicit values inherent in the hospital culture seem to have the greatest impact, and the formal values within the ethical guidelines appear to have the least impact (Hunt, 2004).

Research points to the possibility of a significant difference between formal ethical rules and the prevailing culture within professional occupations. And the development of self-professional identity can be a long-lasting process. These are important factors when exercising value-based leadership over professionals. It is necessary to work on the relations between the espoused values (formal value platforms) and the value-in-use (tacit values within the culture of a profession), with a special focus on young professionals and graduates. These people stand in an intermediate position and can be carriers of both sets of values.

3.5   Summary

Professional values are key to the identity of professionals. They represent both a code of behaviour and also have a strong ethical dimension.

Beck Jørgensen and Bozeman (2007) identified a total of 72 values and organized them into seven categories. These can be viewed as a "public universe of values."

These enable the socialization of individuals within the profession and also serve to regulate entry to the profession and form a justification for disciplining or expelling members of the profession. Stability over time is important for professional identity and so the values espoused by professions tend to be resistant to change. The value bases of service-based professionals will typically focus upon a duty to the client or beneficiary of the profession's skills.

There are strong ethical aspects to professional values and codes but the values tend to be broader than the ethical aspects. Proximity ethics tend to play a key role in healthcare and social-care professions. Examples of professional ethics and codes are widely found and, indeed, in some cases exist across national boundaries. Codes of conduct are frequently found in professions and examples of these are discussed in this chapter.

Professional Identity has a weaker theoretical base than organizational identity but both derive from similar bases. Stability over time and cultural aspects are common to both. Professional identity is not just created through education but also through ongoing practice of the occupation and membership of "communities of practice" such as professional associations. Though there are client-based and ethical value sets, it should not be forgotten that professionals typically also possess a strong self-interest which manifests itself in seeking control over entry to the profession and the maintenance of professional status and accrued rights.

Exercises for further development and understanding

- Consider the changes that have been taken place in the public sector over the last 10–20 years. Discuss if any of the public values have been affected by these changes.
- Which of the values in the public sector do you consider to be most important? Try to place the public values in a hierarchy – the most important values on top and the less important ones at the bottom.
- Picture a profession which you are personally familiar with. Write down the values that in your opinion are related to this profession. Do you consider that any of these values have been changed during recent years?

- Picture a profession which you are familiar with. Describe some of the ethical dilemmas which may occur in this profession. What kind of ethical theories would you recommend to use in the profession in order to develop a professional ethical behaviour?
- Picture a profession that you are familiar with. Describe the professional identity that in your opinion exists in this profession. To what degree do you consider that this identity has a strong value base?

Recommended further reading

Beck Jørgensen, T. & Bozeman, B. (2007). "Public Values. An Inventory," *Administration & Society*, 39, 3, 354–381.

Hatch, M.J. & Schultz, M. (2002). "The Dynamics of Organizational Identity," *Human Relations*, 55, 989–1018.

Schein, E. (2010). *Organizational Culture and Leadership* (4. utg.). San Francisco, CA: Jossey Bass.

Wenger, E. (1998). *Communities of Practice. Learning, Meaning and Identity*. Cambridge: Cambridge University Press.

Values – a conceptual refinement

4

Key learning points

At the end of this chapter the reader should be able to:

- understand how values affect and influence individuals, groups, and the wider society
- appreciate the nature of terminal and instrumental values and their emotional and motivational dimensions
- be aware of the importance of levels at which values are held and appreciate the importance of a hierarchy of values implying some sort of ranking
- understand the way in which values may cluster and that there may be different rationalities coming into play
- understand how values and culture relate to each other especially at the societal and organizational level.

Neither a society nor an organization can function well without a set of shared values. Shared values create confidence and trust, make it possible to live together in harmony, and make it easier to come to decisions. The range of action is reduced and alternatives that violate core values are not an option. Hence, values affect our behaviour to a large extent. This is especially important to professionals in the public sector. Many of their work assignments are unstructured, and they must use their judgement and expertise to solve complex challenges. Society can therefore be regarded as a universe of values containing a host of policies for action; for example, from not jumping red lights to voting in elections. This does not mean that everyone has the same values, or that everyone follows the same standards of conduct, but most people have an insight into what values dominate in society. Moreover, people generally know that sanctions can be brought to bear on actions that violate values. An awareness of which values dominate in an organization is therefore necessary in order to exercise what we call value-based leadership.

4.1   What is a value?

Values are important in a variety of disciplines, such as economics, philosophy, sociology, psychology, and anthropology – which means that the concept of content has a multitude of definitions, although many of them have some common characteristics (Klenke, 2005):

- Values are considered as latent constructs that affect the individual's assessment of activities and results.
- Values are more general than specific in nature.
- Values can be found at different levels.

A value as a latent concept means that there is an underlying concept influencing the individuals' assessments without individuals necessarily being aware of it. Many people can, for example, treat their fellow human beings with great respect without necessarily reflecting on which values constitute the basis for this treatment. Since values are more general than specific, they can cover a broader base. A value tied to treating fellow humans with respect can apply to many situations, such as within the family, in relations to colleagues, towards the users of public services, or in relation to all people a particular person is meeting. Furthermore, general values can more easily be interpreted as relevant for new situations. The last point indicates that values may materialize at several levels. Thus, we can distinguish between individual values, group values, and organizational values.

When values are associated with different professions, it may be useful to distinguish between the *terminal values* and *instrumental values.* Terminal values are linked to a finished state, while the instrumental values are associated with a particular action (Rokeach, 1976). Terminal values represent desirable conditions for a person or a social group. The instrumental values by contrast indicate that certain behaviours are preferable, and thus regulate organizational behaviour. Basically, these values have no value themselves; they are valued only according to their influence on the terminal values (Bozeman, 2007).

In practice it may be difficult to make a clear distinction between terminal values and instrumental values. What constitutes a goal on one level can be a means on another level. At a school, a good class environment can be perceived as an important terminal value. At the same time, developing a healthy class environment is an important means to achieve good class learning. We then bring in an instrumental dimension to this value. A given value can therefore have both a terminal dimension and an instrumental dimension.

It is also possible that an instrumental value completely changes character and develops into a terminal value. At a school it can, for example, be useful to have silence during class as a way to facilitate good learning processes. Here, "silence during class" is an instrumental value and "good learning processes" is a terminal value. When an instrumental value like this persists for a long time, it can change character and become an independent terminal value. This means that the "silence during class" is no longer justified by silence contributing to good learning processes. Then the value itself has changed character and gained a strong terminal dimension.

If an instrumental value changes character in this way, it is no longer possible to determine whether it is functional of dysfunctional – it cannot be empirically tested. Thus, a value like "silence during class" makes it difficult to open up the possibility of noise in class – even though this in itself can be wanted in order to create a particular form of learning. After a review of different approaches to the concept of values, Kluckhohn (1951) emphasizes that a value has three key dimensions:

1. Cognitive
2. Emotional
3. Motivational.

First, values are a *mental construction*; that is, they have a cognitive basis and represent a concept that cannot be observed directly. Hence, it must be possible to convey to others what a certain value consists of. As an example, we can look at the value of respect for other people. In an educational context, it must be possible to discuss what this term means. What do we mean with respect, and in which situations is this value valid? In other words, the values of a society or an organization must be able to be described.

Second, values have an *emotional dimension* – that is, behaviours in conflict with important values create negative emotional reactions. If respect for others is an important value, disrespectful treatment will create anger, frustration, and aggression. In the same way, people behaving in line with the values will create positive feelings in their environment, pointing to the emotional importance of value compliance. Emotions are important in all organizations, and they have a significant impact on the energy generated. We can see this more clearly when there is a struggle over which values should dominate, or when professionals find that their basic values are not sufficiently taken into account. This creates strong emotional reactions and commitments from all concerned, suggesting that values have a positive and a negative side, and we may talk about what is *wrong* and what is *right*. The use of these keywords thus indicates that we are in a value-laden discussion. It is not sufficient that we are able to formulate a value as a mental construction. In order for it to be valuable for us, it must also contain an emotional connection.

The last point indicates that values influence our actions – that they have a *motivational dimension*. Values form the basis for a choice between available methods, means, and ends. This is a key dimension in the concept of value. Values which are internalized have a self-regulatory function by setting a personal standard of behaviour. This has two effects. Firstly, key terminal values will represent important goals to be achieved. Goal attainment will be a reward that can help establish a strong motivation in the work. At a school, for example, a teacher who values knowledge will work diligently to educate students. And employees at a day-care centre may work systematically in an effort to develop children's social skills. Secondly, the instrumental values function as professional standards, where employees are highly motivated to follow these rules. They will exercise a form of self-control as a way to avoid situations where they, through their own behaviour, will challenge their instrumental values. These three dimensions are illustrated in Figure 4.1.

Another important characteristic of values is that they can be both *explicit* and *implicit* (Kluckhohn, 1951). An explicit value means that we have given it a term, making it easy to identify and fill with content. Democracy is an example of an explicit value. This is a central concept in the language, is frequently used, and is relevant in a host of different contexts – from the organization of society to relations within a specific family. Most people also have a relatively clear understanding of what this value consist of. By contrast, an implicit value is not put into words. We may not have a common term for the value, even though the value itself might be an important prerequisite for our behaviour. The individuals within a social group can thus act in line with the values that, linguistically speaking, are not identified. All individuals within an organization, for example, can act respectfully towards each other without having discussed respect for others as a value. This is all right as long as the value is shared by all. If, however, an individual starts acting disrespectfully, it may be necessary to identify the value in order to be able to discuss how employees should treat each other. In a number of organizations, formal value platforms are made as an attempt to highlight important values. By making

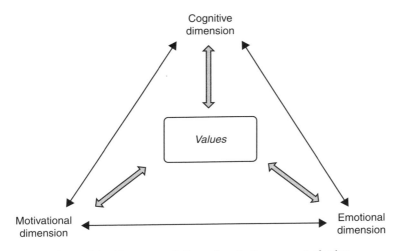

Figure 4.1 Three central dimensions in the concept of value

values explicit, it is easier to work consciously on developing values within the organization.

An element which is also important to highlight is that values are often distinct features of an individual or a social group. This assumes that values are visible and to some extent part of an individual's or a group's identity. It must be noted that even if a value is always linked to a person, we can still talk about a group's or an organization's values. In this context values are given distinct character because of the large extent to which they are shared by all members of the group.

A number of conditions must be present for values to influence behaviour. This especially applies to commitment, trust, and feedback (Thyssen, 2009). A high level of *commitment* contributes to ensuring that employees live by the values present in the organization. They take into account not only their own interests, but also the community they are a part of. *Trust* is also important. A high degree of trust is a key part of the psychological contract between employees and the organization. A trusting relationship between the two gives the employees more freedom to exercise those behaviours that are most appropriate. This also creates a greater degree of accountability. *Feedback* means that learning opportunities are constructed by individuals or groups given the opportunity to reflect on the extent to which they live by their values. This results in a higher level of consciousness, both in terms of central values and in terms of their own behaviour.

It is important to point out that the definition emphasizes the possibility of performing a behaviour that is in line with each individual's own values. The choice is between *available* methods, means, and ends. There are a wide range of factors within an organization that influence employee behaviour. An employment contract regulates what to do, employees are subject to an authority with the power to reward and sanction, and there are a number of rules for what is or is not permissible. As a consequence of this, employees may in a specific situation be forced to exercise a behaviour that is in poor compliance with their own values. A medical doctor may be forced to put patients on a waiting list, although this goes against the doctor's own values of always focusing on the patient's needs first. A welfare worker may be required to transfer a child to an institution, although the worker's individual values indicate that a foster home would be much better for the child. If employees are given little room for practising a behaviour that is in harmony with their individual values, this can reduce both motivation and identification with their organization.

In addition to external rules and injunctions, incentive systems to reduce the link between own values and behaviour can also be established. This means that there is a reward large enough to encourage employees to choose to downgrade their individual values. For example, a university that prioritizes financial rewards to academic staff for publishing research results may reduce the priority given to teaching and student contact, even though the employees believe that learning and developing knowledge among students are important.

Therefore, individual values are of greatest significance in situations where behaviour is marginally impacted by external regulation. This means that employees have a high degree of freedom in their work performance, which is a distinctive feature in most professions. In addition to internalized values influencing individual behaviour, they also form the basis for social control. This applies to both terminal values and instrumental values. Persons who do not appreciate the dominant values will be subjected to social sanctions from their colleagues, assuming that others can observe the behaviour. In other words, social control works only when the behaviour is practised in the social sphere, while self-control also regulates the behaviour that is practised in the private sphere.

Example 7

General MacArthur

The values of West Point
General MacArthur was a career soldier and famous general in the US Army. He was heavily influenced by the values instilled in him by his education at West Point Military Academy, and this excerpt from his farewell speech at West Point perhaps encapsulates a view of such values:

> Duty, Honor, Country: Those three hallowed words reverently dictate what you ought to be, what you can be, what you will be. They are your rallying points: to build courage when courage seems to fail; to regain faith when there seems to be little cause for faith; to create hope when hope becomes forlorn ... these are some of the things they do. They build your basic character. They mold you for your future roles as the custodians of the nation's defense. They make you strong enough to know when you are weak, and brave enough to face yourself when you are afraid.
>
> They teach you to be proud and unbending in honest failure, but humble and gentle in success; not to substitute words for action; not to seek the path of comfort, but to face the stress and spur of difficulty and challenge; to learn to stand up in the storm, but to have compassion on those who fall; to master yourself before you seek to master others; to have a heart that is clean, a goal that is high; to learn to laugh, yet never forget how to weep; to reach into the future, yet never neglect the past; to be serious, yet never take yourself too seriously; to be modest so that you will remember the simplicity of true greatness; the open mind of true wisdom, the meekness of true strength.
>
> They give you a temperate will, a quality of imagination, a vigor of the emotions, a freshness of the deep springs of life, a temperamental predominance of courage over timidity, an appetite for adventure over love of ease. They create in your heart the sense of wonder, the unfailing hope of what next, and the joy and inspiration of life. They teach you in this way to be an officer and a gentleman.[1]

---

[1] Source: http://www.nationalcenter.org/MacArthurFarewell.html accessed 20 Sept 2013

4.2   How are values organized?

Most people have a broad set of values that affect a number of aspects of life. In this context, an interesting question looks at how these values are linked together or organized. Insight into the organization of values is especially important when they are pulled into a leadership process. At that point it is necessary to highlight which values are the most important, and determine if any values build on other values, if there are any conflicting values, or if there are values that are especially relevant in a given work context.

Organizing hierarchically

When it comes to the organization of values, there are many researchers who argue that values are hierarchically organized according to the importance for each individual (Meglino & Ravlin, 1998). In other words, a person has one or a few values with special importance and which are superior to other values. Some may claim that love and care are two superior values, while others prefer justice and equality. At the next level down in the hierarchy are the values that are of lesser importance. At the bottom are the values of least importance for the individual person.

Many organizations develop value platforms, and usually they are based on this type of mindset. A municipality, for example, has chosen to emphasize openness, competence, and courageousness. The idea is that these values should be interpreted within the municipal sector and constitute a basis for more specific values at a lower level. If we take a closer look at this municipality, we find that a nursery has chosen the values of tolerance, compassion, and respect as their most important assets, while a school has selected safety, respect, predictability, transparency, and the right to an active and meaningful life. A hierarchy of values has developed – values that are directly related to the municipality's formal organization of values.

Instead of studying formal value platforms, it is possible to ask employees to list which values are the most important in their job. In a survey among managers in a major Norwegian municipality, the values were ranked as follows (Busch & Wennes, 2012):

1. Professional standards
2. Compliance with the individual user's needs
3. Legal rights
4. Loyalty towards policy decisions
5. Renewal and innovation
6. A general social responsibility.

This does not represent the ranking of a person's values, but shows which values the municipal's unit managers see as the most important. It also forms a sort of hierarchy, even though there is only one value at each level.

In a more fundamental way, public values can be classified according to the rationality or the principle they are based on (Hodgkinson, 1996). This forms a general value hierarchy that is based less on an individual's assessments. At the top level we find the values which are based on fundamental principles. These are values anchored in society; they are largely institutionalized and followed as a sense of duty. Examples include values related to religion or central institutions within the state. The latter can be values such as justice, equality, and loyalty to the political authorities.

At the next level are values based on a rational rationale. They have emerged because they are appropriate. Many of the values associated with professional workers are located at this level and set professional standards for professional conduct. Although these values are largely internalized by professional employees, they can easily be changed if found to have dysfunctional aspects. At the bottom level are values based on individual preferences. They have a more emotional basis and are values that individuals feel drawn towards in a given situation. The values associated with New Public Management can be placed in this group (Beck-Jørgensen, 2007). Examples include performance management, outsourcing, and decentralization. These are new ways of organizing the public sector which have become widespread, although these methods also contain a certain element of fashion (Røvik, 2007). While these new ways may be preferred today, it is unclear to what extent they will be used tomorrow. Figure 4.2 below illustrates these new methods for organizing values.

Such a categorization of values can be ambiguous and values may flow through all three levels. A value currently based on personal preferences can move up in the hierarchy and in a later phase have a more rational basis, at the end being internalized as a pillar of the society. Or conversely, a value previously built on a strong sense of duty may lose its fundamental character and move downwards in the hierarchy. Within value-based leadership, it is important to discuss which values are fundamental and which values are more situation-dependent. This

Grounds of value	Examples
Principles	Justice Equality Loyalty
Rational rationale	User orientation Care Efficiency
Personal preference	Outsourcing Performance management Balanced scorecard

Figure 4.2   Value hierarchy in the public sector

can provide managerial flexibility which in turn can provide a larger organizational capacity for change. At the same time, it can be necessary to consider which values are in motion within the organization. If key values are in motion, it may be beneficial to focus on these rather than on the values that are stable and well internalized among the employees.

Organizing in clusters

A hierarchical organization of values is not without complications. For the most part, it requires values to be organized within a coherent structure; something which does not capture the fact that different values can be separated from each other (Kluckhohn, 1951). An alternative is to assume that values are organized in clusters (Beck-Jørgensen, 2003a, 2006). On this basis, values that belong to the same cluster are to a large extent uniform and integrated, while at the same time there can be large distances between the different clusters. Within each cluster, there may be a dominant value, known as a nodal value. Around the nodal values we find the neighbour values. These are values which are strongly associated with the nodal values, but with a different significance. For example, we may find the following clusters of values at a hospital:

- *Economic*. Here we can find values associated with productivity, efficiency, fiscal discipline, and so on. A nodal value can be efficiency.
- *Democratic*. Values here may be associated with the basic democratic organization of society. Relevant values can be justice, equality, and loyalty to political decisions. A nodal value can be justice.
- *Professional*. Several professions are represented at a hospital, and several professional clusters may be present. Among the nurses, we may find values like altruism, care, respect, and participation. A nodal value can also be altruism.

We may also find other value clusters at a hospital. This may be a bureaucratic cluster, where we find values like orderliness, accuracy, and loyalty to the rules, or an HRM (human resource management) cluster, with values related to creating a good and meaningful work environment for employees. Values can be soundly integrated within each cluster; that is, they function as a whole where the individual values support each other. If one value has to be changed, all the other values in this cluster will probably have to be adjusted as well.

What characterize a nodal value are its close ties to the majority of the other values in the cluster. To obtain an overview of possible value clusters within an organization, a systematic analysis is therefore required. First, all relevant values must be identified, and then the values that appear to have a strong presence need to be pinpointed. This will indicate which clusters exist. The value within each cluster that appears to have the most ties to the other values must be identified. This constitutes a nodal value, and the others can then be defined as neighbouring values.

Organizing values in clusters reveals built-in conflicts between the different clusters or values. Professional values may be in conflict with values related to the economy or bureaucracy. If a doctor has values connected to all three of these value clusters, she may experience a dilemma: no matter what she does, she may contravene one of the values which steers her work. Within a strict budget, it can be hard to provide individual treatment and at the same time of-fer everyone the same treatment. At a school, teachers can experience a dilemma between spending time on documentation (bureaucratic rule) and spending time on students (professional rule).

This can lead to a decoupling of values (Beck-Jørgensen, 2003a, 2006); that is, a person is unable to see the values in context. In this sense, values are only activated in situations where they are relevant to particular tasks. The professional values related to the teaching profession, for example, may only be activated in a teaching situation. And when the same teacher makes his reports to document the students' development, only the bureaucratic val-ues are enabled. Thus, the teacher avoids value conflicts. Another possibility is, of course, that value conflicts lead to a failure to internalize some values. Professional employees can, for example, reject all values that are not in accor-dance with their profession. This is illustrated in Figure 4.3. Here, three value clusters are identified: bureaucratic, professional, and economic. The question marks and lines indicate uncertainty about the degree of coupling or decou-pling between these clusters of value.

To illustrate conflicts between values or value clusters, it is possible to orga-nize values on a circle (Swartz, 1992). Values located on either side of the circle are in conflict with each other, whereas values that are placed next to each other on the circle are in harmony. To perform this analysis, it is necessary to work

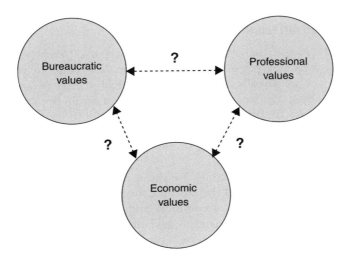

Figure 4.3   Coupling between the three value clusters

only with a limited number of values. Based on this, we can analyse the potential value conflicts between different clusters by studying the relations between the nodal values in each relevant cluster. We can also study the relations between other values of an organization or social group. This can be a value platform designed to highlight the most important values. Such an analysis will increase awareness of the potential value conflicts within the organization.

Example 8

Values in a hospital setting

In a major UK hospital there were major concerns raised about the standard of care of patients. Well over 1,000 patients were deemed to have died as a direct or indirect consequence of poor standards of care at the hospital over fewer than 5 years. The hospital had, during the period of concern, managed to achieve Foundation status which was seen at the time as a measure of confidence in its standards. However, a focus on particular central targets was seen as having led to a neglect of basic values of care and compassion. Patients had been left without access to food and water, and those unable to feed themselves had suffered as a consequence. Perhaps significantly, the concerns had been raised not so much by staff as by the relatives of the patients.

A succession of inquiries led to a general view that an obsession with targets had eroded the more critical human values which were seen as essential in nursing and basic care. Suggestions were made that increasing the formal educational requirements and training of nurses needed to be balanced by a return to the caring values inculcated by hands-on experience and a return to the standards espoused the professional values of nurses.

4.3   Values at different levels

We previously argued that values can be grouped at different levels. This is a perspective which is particularly important in leadership of professionals. Although values are initially linked to an individual, it may be appropriate to talk about values on higher levels. This means that a group of people can share one or more values. In principle, it may here be useful to distinguish between society, profession, organization, workgroup, and individuals. In practice, of course, people will be members of several groups which to a varying degree share the same values.

One may argue that social values are those that are shared by the majority in a society or in a nation, and the basis for them may be linked to a common religion, a common history, or a common language. One may also argue that many values are global, being linked to the core of what it means to be human; for example, care and respect. The term "institution" allows us to describe social values and operates as a guideline that governs the behaviour of individuals. Every society has a number of institutions with a value basis. These institutions operate as the unwritten rules of accepted behaviour. Here, we find a host of guidelines for what is accepted as ethically and morally acceptable behaviour.

All organizations must adapt to the values that dominate in society (Selznick, 1957). At a retirement home, for example, it is expected that the residents be treated with courtesy and respect, and that their need for privacy is taken into account. At a school, it is expected that the teachers work to create a good learning environment and prevent student bullying. If the organization breaks the unwritten rules of society, it loses its legitimacy and will be subject to sanctions by the political authorities. When the organizations gradually adapt to the values in society, they will receive a value-based status. This means that the organization is no longer simply seen as a tool that can be replaced as needed, but instead acquires value of its own.

This process is particularly important for organizations with diffuse goals and unclear technology; for example, public and voluntary organizations. The Red Cross is, for example, perceived by most people to be a carrier of important values in our society, and it has a high level of legitimacy as a consequence. The same applies to hospitals, retirement homes, and schools. It is difficult to measure how effective these organizations are, and it is unclear what the best way of achieving their goals is. However, their legitimacy is not necessarily a function of their effectiveness, but of the value they have in their own right. This means that many of the values that exist in the society will be established in individual organizations over time.

In addition, a distinct culture is created in most organizations. This distinct culture will, among other things, be affected by the tasks to be performed (Schein, 2010). Therefore, we find different organizational cultures in hospitals to those in schools – even though many of their values are the same. There are also large differences in public, voluntary, and private establishments. In short, organizations in society will be both carriers of common values and develop their own unique organizational cultures.

It is also meaningful to talk about values at the group level – meaning common values developed in a smaller group or a subculture in an organization. It is likewise important to note that the values found in a group to a large extent reflect the values of society or the organization that the group belongs to. The development of specific group values derives from situations where the community has experienced and solved significant social problems (Schein, 2010). It is especially important that the group has shared emotional experiences such as joy, happiness, anxiety, aggression, etc. These conditions will quickly create a sense of community. Looking at a school, for instance, a team of educators will be able to fill these conditions. Based on various subjects, the team will work together to create a good classroom environment, positive learning processes, and good academic results. They will face many challenges and problems to be solved, and there is some replacement of members. This applies to many groups within the public professions – whether they work within education, health, social services, or other sorts of welfare production.

Although we are talking about values at an aggregated level, the values always anchor to the individual. Our personal values are mainly created through a socialization process. A child will, through education and other social influences, quickly learn both instrumental values and terminal values. Upbringing involves both shaping behaviour and teaching the child to appreciate certain aspects of life. Often, values developed during upbringing have an either-or characteristic (Rokeach, 1973). Being polite, for example, applies to all situations – politeness is either a value or it is not a value. There is nothing in-between.

This process continues in the school system, where the students must learn to function in larger social contexts and obtain additional training in how to articulate the central values of society. In a vocational education, the values associated with that specific profession are taught. Taken together, when the student enters the workforce, he or she is already equipped with a set of values both tailored to the society and to the profession chosen to make a career in. Yet students are not simply empty vessels waiting to be socialized. Indeed, research has shown that an individual can influence socialization processes (Bauer et al., 1998), especially in relation to a new job. Through experiences, expertise, skills, and personality, a person can influence their own degree of socialization. The fact that the socialization process evolves more easily when there is a substantial similarity between personal values and organizational values has also been established (Chatman, 1991).

Thus, we can draw a line from the individual and up to a social level. We are not alone with our values. They are shared by many others and created in all social contexts. The differences at the individual level disappear when we shift our view to the social level. And even if there are a host of different organizational cultures and professional cultures in a society, more similarities than differences are present.

4.4 Summary

Shared values are key to the functioning of groups, organizations, and, in particular, society in general. They create confidence and trust. They are found at different levels and take on difference characteristics. In particular, it is important to distinguish between terminal and instrumental values. Values are seen as having cognitive, emotional, and motivational dimensions.

Thus, values can be both functional and dysfunctional and have motivational importance. They influence our actions. Sometimes values are made explicit; for example, in formal statements or codes of practice. However, they may also be implicit and not written down but rather discovered from their application in use. Conditions such as level of commitment and feedback and trust are also important. Reference in this chapter is also made to methods and means which encompass incentive systems.

Values are usually structured in a hierarchical fashion with some values having a superordinate importance. They may also be determined by a particular rationality – be it professional, social or economic – which can lead to value clusters. Values are also found at different levels in organizations and in society at large.

Exercises for further development and understanding

- Identify what values you would regard as commonly held in the society in which you live. How do these compare to values in other societies which you may have experienced or visited. Are there differences, and if so what do you think may account for them?
- In your work setting (or one you have experienced), identify a situation where there has been a clash of values. A situation where two values are competing and pulling (or pushing) in different directions. How was the clash resolved and what lessons do you draw from this?
- How may a manager who is also a professional resolve conflicting values? Perhaps the professional value argues for a particular resource to be committed but the managerial/organizational values suggest a different path.
- Should societal values take precedence over and determine professional values?

Recommended further reading

Beck-Jørgensen, T. (2006). "Value Consciousness and Public Management," *International Journal of Organization Theory and Behavior*, 9, 510–536.

Rokeach, M. (1976). "The Nature of Human Values and Value Systems," in Hollander, E.P. & Hunt, R.G. (eds) *Current Perspectives in Social Psychology*. New York: Oxford University Press.

Part 2
Leadership in a value-based perspective

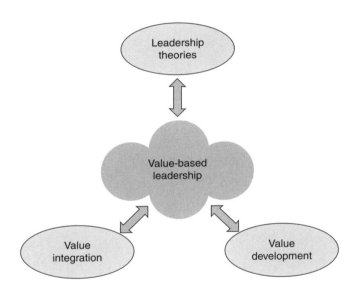

Value-based leadership is not just about working with the values. It is also necessary to focus on the leadership function. Therefore, values must be integrated with the leadership processes and directed towards realizing important goals. Part 2 firstly contains a brief introduction to the development of leadership theory and then moves on to parse out a conceptual model for value-based leadership. Here, the first emphasis is on showing how leadership can be anchored in a solid value base. Part 2 ends by reviewing the various methods that can be used to work with value development. Here, we will also discuss whether it is desirable to change employees' values and how leaders should handle conflicting values in their own organizations.

A theoretical starting point for leadership

5

Key learning points

At the end of this chapter the reader should be able to:

- appreciate the complexity of leadership as a theoretical concept
- understand the variety of theories which are used to explain leadership
- be aware of the characteristics of the New Public Leadership
- understand the major challenges that political leaders face
- understand the origins of value-based leadership and be aware of the principal dimensions in ethical and authentic leadership.

Leadership is perceived as a complex phenomenon. So far a coherent and well-established paradigm in leadership research has not been developed. There are a number of theories and definitions that emphasize different aspects of the leadership process. Most definitions of leadership reflect an intentional process exercised by a person in an effort to manage the activities and relationships in a group or organization. However, there is considerable disagreement as to whether or not leadership should be tied to specific roles or be considered as a process aimed at exercising influence (Yukl, 2006). In order to develop a model that captures value-based leadership over professional employees, it is first necessary to choose a leadership theory to use. Without a concrete leadership theory, value-based leadership will lose its intentional dimension – that is, the leadership concept is not tied to the realization of goals. Value-based leadership will then be reduced to working with values and developing values. This is important, but it cannot be regarded as leadership. In this chapter we will outline some of the leadership theories that can be used as a basis for developing a model for value-based leadership.

5.1   Personal attributes of leaders

Scientists have long been committed to identifying what characterizes good leadership, which in this context means that leadership contributes to achieving organizational goals. To identify this, definitions first emphasized the personality traits of leaders. Previous studies pinpointed a number of personality traits. However, thorough research showed that these explanations were too simple. Recent research has indicated that some traits seem to have a positive impact on the organization's or group's effectiveness (Yukl, 2006):

- high energy level and stress tolerance
- self-confidence
- internal locus of control orientation
- emotional stability and maturity
- personal integrity
- socialized power motivation
- moderately high achievement orientation
- low need for affiliation.

Furthermore, possessing relational, cognitive, and technical skills has proven to be advantageous. Relational skills involve managing relations between people. This means the ability to understand how emotions, attitudes, and motivation affect the relations within a group, and the skills to work with these factors. Cognitive skills are related to logical intelligence and ability to manage complex situations. Technical skills are related to knowledge of the technology that dominates in the organization. Emotional and social intelligence have also been shown to be of importance.

These theories point to a number of dimensions that may be of importance for understanding the leadership of professionals. In particular, the theories can point out potential causes for the appearance of leadership problems in an organization. At the same time, they may be difficult to operationalize since personal qualities are not easy to alter: it may be a challenge to improve the leadership processes by addressing and changing personal qualities. Skills are somewhat different, as skills can be taught – for example, through leadership development programmes.

To insert these theories into a value-based perspective, we need to ask if the leader's value base has any significance for the quality of leadership. It is well documented how a leader's values can influence his or her leadership behaviour. Yet it is difficult to prove that specific values themselves contribute to improving leadership efficiency. An interesting research finding, however, is that successful leaders have the same values as those being led (Bass, 2008), indicating that value-based leadership has something to offer leadership theory.

5.2   Styles of leadership

Due to the weak results produced by research related to personality theories, a new research tradition has emerged, where the focus is set on the leader's actions instead of on the leader's personal characteristics. A number of leadership behaviours have been studied, revealing that actions can often be tied to two underlying behavioural dimensions. Although there are some variations with respect to what these entail, they are largely related to:

1. *The leader's task orientation.* That is, the extent to which the leaders focus on solving the organization's task, emphasizing management and control.
2. *The leader's relational orientation.* That is, the extent to which the leaders focus on the relations between the employees performing the tasks, emphasizing care and consideration.

Leadership style may in this context be defined as leaders managing a balance between these two behavioural dimensions. Early studies examined which of these two dimensions were most effective, showing that effective leaders were much more relation-oriented when compared to ineffective leaders (Likert, 1979). They were more thoughtful and concerned about others as people, including concern over their feelings, needs, and social conditions. Further research indicated that it was more accurate to view the task orientation and relational orientation as two independent dimensions (Blake & Mouton, 1964). This means that a leader can have both strong task orientation and strong relational orientation. It was thus possible to outline numerous combinations of scores on these two dimensions.

It was hard to prove which of these complex leadership styles were most effective, and attention was eventually paid to the context or situation in which leadership was exercised (Tannenbaum & Schmidt, 1958). The basic conclusion reached was that no leadership style in itself is the best one. Instead, it is the leader's overall situation that determines what leadership style to select. In one situation it may be appropriate to use a more task-oriented leadership style. In another situation, it is best to focus on involving the employees. It then becomes important for the leader to correctly diagnose the situation. In doing so, leadership must adapt to: (a) the leader himself and his value system; (b) the employees; and (c) the actual situation or task to be solved.

The leader himself

Personal qualities set limitations on which leadership style can be used. A leader who has always worked in close interaction with his employees will have difficulty switching to a more task-oriented leadership style – even if the situation requires it. Based on this, a leader should look for situations which are well adapted to his personal characteristics and preferences. Among other things, the leader's value system is of great importance. This means that it is difficult to exercise a form of leadership that is in opposition to one's values. A leader who has strong values related to participation, involvement, and care for employees can have difficulties exercising a form of authoritarian leadership.

Employees

When it comes to employees, their level of maturity and commitment to organizational goals are key factors. Maturity can in this context be defined as the ability to set high but attainable goals, the willingness and ability to assume responsibility, and possessing the requisite knowledge and experience (Schein, 1988). In this area there are different theories which recommend different leadership styles as employees develop from novices to experts (Hersey & Blanchard, 1977). If maturity is low, the leader should be exercising strong governance. As maturity increases, the leader should reduce her governing behaviour and increasingly support the employees in their professional development. In the end, the leader should slightly pull herself out of the relationship with the employees and instead facilitate an arena for employee self-leadership.

The situation or task to be solved

The actual situation or task to be solved can also be crucial for which leadership style is effective. In the case of the general situation, organizational culture is especially significant. This will often lead to an emerging pressure where leaders are expected to behave according to the prevailing values of an organization. For example, if an authoritarian headmaster is employed in a secondary school, and the school is characterized by democratic values, conflicts can quickly emerge. The leader's behaviour must therefore be adapted to the expectations inherent in the organizational culture. When it comes to the tasks, the complexity is of great importance (Vroom & Yetton, 1973). It is vital that the employees are actively involved in the process of very complex tasks. The same applies to tasks that require a great deal of creativity and innovation. In this case, an environment must be developed where employees are involved and can influence the process.

5.3   Public leadership theories

Efforts have also been made to develop leadership theories specifically for the public sector. Focusing on the public context and the challenges faced by public-sector leaders, these theories pay less attention to what characterizes leadership behaviour. In this chapter we take a closer look at the New Public Leadership concept, and at political leadership.

New Public Leadership

The concept of New Public Leadership (NPL) represents a critique of New Public Management (NPM), which has dominated public-sector development over the past three decades (Brookes & Grint, 2010). More explicitly, the focus has shifted from management to leadership among key political actors. Brookes and Grint (2010) consider the concept of leadership better suited when dealing with the complexities found in the public sector, describing the differences between NPL and NPM thus:

1. NPL is better adapted to the context than NPM.
2. NPL has a stronger focus on network organization.
3. Since its scope is wider, NPL creates greater "public value" than NPM.

The most important perspective in Brookes and Grint (2010) is the strong collective dimension of NPL: management responsibilities extend beyond their own organization. This is in line with increasing criticism of NPM from a network perspective in recent years. A main point here is that NPM has led to greater fragmentation of the public sector, thus reducing the possibility of finding comprehensive solutions (Christensen & Lægreid, 2007). The background is that increasing deregulation and creation of new bodies have resulted in a polycentric society (Sand, 2004). It has therefore become more difficult to deal with cross-disciplinary and cross-sectoral problems – so-called "wicked problems."

These developments have created a need for what is described as collective leadership. The concept involves two dimensions: horizontal and vertical (Brookes & Grint, 2010). In the horizontal dimension, organizations must co-operate to solve joint problems; in the vertical dimension, the management must ensure good results in their own organization. The horizontal dimension indicates that public institutions need to establish networks in order to solve key challenges facing the welfare state. Such networks can include other public organizations, private enterprises, and voluntary organizations. They can be classified according to their main function (Klijn, 2008):

1. *Political networks* aimed at acquiring power and influence over decision processes. This type of network involves political actors.
2. *Inter-organizational networks* aimed at service production and policy implementation. These networks are regarded as important instruments in the efficient production of complex welfare services, and in the implementation of difficult political decisions.
3. *Governance networks* aimed at co-ordinating different actors in order to maximize the functioning of the public sector in a polycentric society.

The fact that these networks differ with regard to functions and properties has an impact on organization and governance as well as leadership. Political networks are relatively closed, and play an important role in political governance at the national, regional, and municipal levels. In contrast, the other networks are more open, while at the same time subject to a greater degree of regulation from above.

An important aspect of NPL is the strong emphasis on public value (Brookes & Grint, 2010). Leaders are expected to retain a focus on the total value creation of the welfare society, and on how they can best contribute to this value creation. Among other things, this means that leaders must focus on long-term goals – requiring strategic leadership aimed at ensuring value creation in the future. In the assessment of public value creation, meeting social goals is considered at least as important as fulfilling the short-term and quantitative goals which play such a dominant role within NPM.

Trust and legitimacy are two important conditions for delivering high public value (Benington & Moore, 2010). A network consists of several equal partners, none of whom has the authority to decide what the network should do and how it should operate. What keeps the network together is trust: a conviction that all parties are dedicated to the common good. Such trust must be built over time, between the individuals brought together by this network, and between the organizations involved.

At the same time, managers and organizations depend on high legitimacy. They need a high degree of social acceptance both for the goals they strive towards, and the means employed to reach these goals. Determining what results contribute to the creation of high public value is not up to the individual manager; it is a matter for political processes involving the active participation of important stakeholders. Hence public organizations can be seen as upholders of central social values, which is key to achieving high legitimacy.

Rather than an alternative to NPM, Brookes and Grint (2010) regard NPL as a necessary supplement. All organizations require both management and governance. However, solving the complex challenges of the future requires a new form of leadership which also promotes horizontal co-operation and seeks to facilitate the development of functional network solutions. If the long-term goals for our welfare society are to be realized, managers must lift their gaze and see that they are part of a larger picture.

Example 9

Haram – a Norwegian council

A small Norwegian council confronted a problem of how to attract and hold people to come and work there and to retain key local employers. The problem reached beyond the normal remit of a council to provide services and political accountability. The solution adopted involved engaging in collective leadership involving politicians from all the parties, the management of the council and also local stakeholders. The council was able to drive forward a major change involving a flattened structure and adopt a new paradigm based on education and collective leadership. The politicians made a commitment to being involved in the learning process and to actively engage with managers in developing a strategic vision to work on the new council plan. The council was able to successfully engage with local employers and work towards the goal of making Haram the "leading maritime and industrial commune in Norway."[1]

---

[1] See Murdock, A. (2008) "Haram: strategic change through education and partnership" (with J.O. Vanebo) in Johnson, G. and Scholes, K. and Whittingdon, R. *Exploring corporate strategy*. Prentice Hall, pp. 840–846.

Political leadership

An important part of public leadership is the leadership that takes place in formal political systems – more particularly the leadership exercised by elected political representatives. These can be defined as: (a) democratic elected representatives who (b) are vulnerable to re-election and are (c) operating within and affect constitutional and legal frameworks (Morrell & Hartley, 2006). Furthermore, their authority and exercise of control is based on the mandate given by voters, who submit their votes based on some form of constitution provisions. Political leadership in this context is an under-researched area (Hartley, 2010). Within political science, little focus is placed on political leadership processes, and within general leadership theory, the particular contexts prevailing in political systems are not given a lot of consideration.

The autonomization and fragmentation of the public sector also place politicians in front of more demanding and complex tasks. Although they have deregulated key public functions, established public companies with extensive autonomy, and delegated authority and responsibility for public services, politicians are still responsible for the actions of these agencies. Instances of "wicked problems" beg for their attention – whether they be within healthcare, transport, or education. Yet politicians increasingly enter network solutions with reduced power and authority. In the same way that public administration must explore new ways to solve complex problems, politicians are also facing new challenges. The polycentric nature of society is not easy to control, and when politicians must engage in various forms of negotiations with private or nongovernmental organizations, the relations between politics and administration can also become blurred. Politicians must engage in more vague and unpredictable processes, and the leadership perspective becomes increasingly important.

Today there is a growing recognition that understanding context is an important prerequisite for determining what kind of leadership is possible to develop within an organization (Porter & McLaughlin, 2006), although there is currently little empirical research focusing on this. Political leadership must be understood within the context in which it is a part, and changes in the context must lead to adjustments of the leadership process. Hartley (2010) specifies five arenas within which local politicians must operate today:

1. Development and support of grassroots movements
2. Negotiation and mobilization of effective partnerships with other public agencies, as well as with private and voluntary organizations
3. Highlighting community needs and interests in regional, national, and international arenas
4. Governance and strategic leadership of public-service organizations;
5. Co-operation within political parties – both locally and nationally in order to develop appropriate political coalitions.

This demonstrates that local politicians will operate in several different contexts, each with its special requirements for what constitutes effective leadership. These complexities increase at the national level, where larger interest groups can be found and where the room for leadership-related action can be challenged. Research has indicated that an effective political leader is one who has the ability to read the current context and customize his or her own leadership to fit the existing requirements and opportunities, while at the same time articulating and adjusting the context (Leach et al., 2005). This means that it is not just a matter of adapting to a context. The context can also be constituted by politicians through opinion-making processes. Within this research, the following leadership tasks appear to be central to local politicians (Hartley, 2010):

- maintaining a critical mass of political support
- developing strategic goals in different policy areas
- influencing leadership priorities outside their own organizations
- ensuring that tasks are executed.

Although these four tasks might be part of nearly any leadership position, they also demonstrate the wide range of tasks a politician must relate to. The first point is perhaps the one that is the most distinct for political leaders. They must always be concerned with securing adequate political support – whether it be within their own party, within a coalition of several parties, or in relation to the voters. This important task may greatly influence the politician's leadership behaviour. The second task – the development of strategic goals – has a different nature and is universal for everyone who exercises leadership at a high level in an organization. In a political context, this task has a particularly close connection with the maintenance of political support. For politicians, it is important to communicate with their supporters by conveying clear visions for future development, which is quite a challenging balancing act. Should the strategic goals be formulated to ensure the support of voters and other supporting players or should they be formulated on the basis of what is considered best for the municipality, region, or nation? These two assessments rarely coincide; their coincidence instead requires good political leadership.

The third point indicates that a politician must also engage in decisions that, while outside his or her area of responsibility, may still be vital to society's development. This might include priorities within larger private companies, within Non-Governmental Organizations (NGOs), or within other political bodies. To influence these priorities, politicians have to be involved in various networks. This means that they must step outside the area in which they have a hierarchical position, and by interacting with other actors, contribute to realizing their strategic goals. The last point – ensuring the execution of tasks – is related to the fact that politicians have a responsibility to implement their policy decisions. Although the implementation is left to the administrators and the welfare producers, the sitting politicians ultimately have the overall responsibility for effective administration and effective service production.

5.4   Value-based leadership

Value-based leadership can largely be traced back to Robert House (1996), who discussed and elaborated on what he called value-based leader behaviour. However, the awareness of leadership as being value-based goes much further back in time. It is a central assumption in Institutional Theory (Selznick, 1957), which assumes that both ends and means have strong value anchoring, especially in public organizations. This is necessary for the organization to have an intrinsic value. Indeed, by complying with the values of society, the organization achieves a symbolic value that extends the organization's primary function. It is no longer just an instrument for producing specific products and services, but attains an independent value that provides the organization with a high level of legitimacy.

Values are also a key element in the theories of bureaucracies; that is, organizational forms characterized by a strong emphasis on formal rules (Weber, 1978). Although the rules to a large extent regulate employee behaviour, leaders need the ability to exercise judgment and make decisions – in other words, they need to exercise discretion. For the bureaucracy to work, it is necessary for the leaders to follow professional and ethical guidelines. There must be an organizational culture that prevents leaders from abusing their power.

House (1996) takes this a step further by connecting value-based leadership to the leader's ability to express a value-based vision that creates a moral commitment among employees. Thus, the values are placed in a leadership perspective. They are not only essential for ensuring the organization's reputation or ensuring that leaders behave in ethical ways. A leader with a value-based perspective is able to express a vision while appealing to employees' central values and unconscious motives, so they become motivated to engage in the organization's overall vision. The consistency between the leader's values and the organization's values is important for success. These conditions have led to value-based leadership being largely associated with transformational leadership and charismatic leadership (MacTavish & Kolb, 2008).

There is also a strong value dimension in theories related to *ethical leadership* (Bass & Steidlmeier, 1999), where strong ethical values are seen as important, and where these values are the basis for leadership decisions in the organization. We find similar claims in the theories of *authentic leadership*, which also has a strong anchoring of the values (Bass, 2008). Yet authentic leadership also sees leaders as being true to themselves; that is, there must be consistency between their own values and their own behaviours. Transformational leadership will be addressed in depth in Chapter 10; here we take a closer look at *ethical leadership* and *authentic leadership*.

Ethical leadership

The ethical dimensions have always been considered important within the literature on leadership (Bass, 2008), and in an age when scandals in the worlds of business and public administration are often of an ethical nature, there has been increasing attention on ethical leadership. Although many of the theories in this area are normative – that is, they specify what constitutes ethical behaviour by a leader or what virtues the leader should possess – empirical research conducted in recent years has also examined how ethical leadership functions in practice (Brown & Treviño, 2006). Ethical leadership is founded on three pillars (Bass & Steidlmeier, 1999):

1. The moral character of the leader
2. The ethical legitimacy of the values embedded in the leader's vision, articulation, and programme
3. The morality of the processes of social ethical choices and actions that leaders and followers engage in and collectively pursue

The leader, then, must possess specific ethical character traits or hold certain values. Important aspects here are integrity, honesty, trustworthiness, fairness, and caring – on an individual as well as a social level (Treviño et al., 2000). In addition, it emerges that the ethical values in question must enjoy high legitimacy, meaning that they must be accepted by society at large as important ethical standards. Finally, certain requirements are made of the decision-making processes and the actions taken in situations of ethical choice – ethical standards must also apply to these.

An important perspective on leadership in these theories is that leaders must actively influence the ethical behaviour of their employees (Brown & Treviño, 2006). In other words, a leader must make ethics an explicit aspect of their leadership behaviour, by communicating ethical values, acting as a good role model, and holding the employees responsible for their ethical or unethical behaviour.

What factors are conducive to ethical leadership in an organization? A review of relevant research literature suggests that three conditions are particularly important (Brown & Treviño, 2006). Firstly, it is important to have good role models. Social learning theory has documented that observing others is on a par with making our own experiences when it comes to learning (Bandura, 1986). We learn by copying the behaviours of others, in other words. It is vital here that the role models hold positions of power or enjoy high social status. The role models must also be easily observable. Key individuals openly embracing ethical behaviour – both through their actions and by verbally expressing the importance of these matters – is therefore a great advantage when seeking to develop ethical leadership in an organization. This allows observers of the behaviour to copy not only the actions, but also the attitudes and cognitive models.

Secondly, it is important that the organization has an ethical culture; in other words, that an organizational culture containing certain ethical values – both terminal and instrumental – has been developed. Furthermore, it is also important that these values are made manifest in a set of ethical rules, thus making them more easily detectable to the staff. In other words, the leadership conducted in an organization must reflect its ethical values. The existence of a strong ethical culture will therefore facilitate ethical leadership.

Finally, ethical leadership will be influenced by the ethical awareness found in an organization; that is, to what extent leaders and staff are capable of detecting or perceiving potential ethical challenges. In situations where errors are expected to have large negative consequences and where there is also a strong ethical culture, ethical awareness is seen to increase.

Ethical leadership, then, is furthered by strong ethical role models, a strong ethical culture, and high ethical awareness. Such leadership can have a positive impact on the organization in terms of ethical behaviour, loyalty, commitment, motivation, and attachment (Brown & Treviño, 2006).

Authentic leadership

Still under development, existing theories on authentic leadership build to some extent on ethical leadership theories (Gardner et al., 2011). To date, there is no authoritative definition of authentic leadership; rather, different definitions emphasize different dimensions of the leadership concept. Authenticity is about a person showing their "real" self, and behaving according to their innermost nature. These are some of the central dimensions in authentic leadership:

1. Consistency between values and actions
2. High self-awareness
3. Strong self-regulation
4. High level of moral development.

High consistency between values and actions means that authentic leaders do not compromise their values (Ryan & Deci, 2003). Rather than adapt to some external form of control – rules, instructions, or orders imposed by their superiors – authentic leaders act according to their own values and beliefs. This can create conflicts, but at the same time it can also help create a greater awareness of the organization's fundamental values.

High self-awareness means that authentic leaders have great insight into their own strengths and weaknesses, and accept these. They know who they are, and they are aware of their own fundamental values. Such individuals also develop high self-esteem – which makes them stable and mature and likely to develop close relationships and to adopt open attitudes to other people (Kernis, 2003). High self-awareness is a prerequisite for being able to act according to one's values.

Strong self-regulation is also necessary in order for authentic leaders to behave according to their own values (Avolio & Gardner, 2005). Their intentions and actions will be adapted to their fundamental values through extensive self-control. An important basis for authentic leadership, this regulatory behaviour is an integrated part of their selves. It requires a balanced assessment of the available information and an open attitude to other people. High self-regulation is an important aspect of self-leadership; for an in-depth discussion of this, see Chapter 8.

The final point indicates that authentic leaders must work according to high ethical standards (Gardner et al., 2005). High moral demands are made of the leaders and their behaviour. Thus, being true to their own values is not enough in itself; their values must also coincide with the ethical standards developed within their profession or in society at large.

We see that authentic leadership has adopted many of the central points from ethical leadership. The greatest difference is the strong focus in the former on leaders being seen to act in keeping with their inner selves: they must be genuine and act according to their inner values. It is not enough, in other words, for leaders to act in a way that is ethical. The ethical values must be internalized; they must be part of the leaders' inner selves.

Several studies have examined the effect of authentic leadership (for a review, see Walumbwa et al., 2010). The results indicate that authentic leaders have a significant amount of influence on staff behaviour. One of the areas impacted by authentic leadership is organizational commitment. Strong commitment means that staff members experience a strong emotional attachment to the organization. There is also a positive correlation between authentic leadership and both job satisfaction and supervision satisfaction. Finally, there are strong indications that authentic leaders have a positive influence on staff performance. In sum, this form of value-based leadership seems to have a positive effect not only for the staff members close to the leaders, but also on the results produced.

Example 10

Nelson Mandela

The film *Invictus* portrays the key importance of symbolic leadership reaching across societal sectors. Nelson Mandela is keenly aware that he is leader of a deeply divided country and that he has to find a way to reach out to the substantial White minority population, many of whom regard him and the new Black African-dominated government negatively. The consequence of failing to successfully reach out to this part of the population would be a failure in the most fundamental need to build a new nation. It also could represent a crucial loss of needed skills and resources in nation building.

The vehicle of sport is where Mandela succeeds with his espousal of the South African rugby team – heavily symbolic of the former Apartheid regime. He realizes the importance of a genuine engagement with the team and the film shows him taking the time to learn about the rules and sporting ethos of the game and also devoting time to personally getting to know the team and in particular building a close relationship with the team captain. Mandela wears the team shirt – in itself a highly symbolic act.

When the South African team wins, the imagery is of a nation coming together and the film portrays the team singing the national anthem of the new South Africa.

5.5   Summary

The concept of leadership has been explored through various theoretical approaches. The trait approach stresses the importance of personality and personal attributes and this has relevance for a value-based approach to leadership. However, considerable weight needs to be attached to the actions which distinguish a leader. This has been encompassed by an approach which examines the style adopted, something which is affected by the context and the importance of matching an appropriate leadership style to the demands of the situation. Yukl (2006) has described a number of traits which are seen as positively related to leader effectiveness.

Style of leadership has emerged as a field of study in response to the limited results attributed to personality theories. Task/relationship orientation is an example of this and is explored in this chapter. The leadership situation or context is also regarded as an important – perhaps crucial – factor.

In the area of public management a new approach focused on NPL is explored using the work of Brooks & Grint (2010) which emphasizes the importance of public value. Network theory has also become important with particular reference to political, inter-organizational and governance networks. Context has become important, and this chapter makes reference to the work of Hartley (2010) who describes various arenas where local politicians need to operate. Hartley identifies various leadership tasks which appear central to politicians.

We argue that a process-based approach is particularly suited to examining a value-based approach. Here we draw upon the work of Erik Johnsen in a Scandinavian context. This stresses the importance of objectives and goal-setting, problem-solving and leadership as a process of language creation. The importance of ethical awareness and leadership leads to a final account of authentic leadership which we regard as an emerging field of leadership which is still under development.

Exercises for further development and understanding

- Consider your experience of various leaders and identify how the various theoretical approaches described in this chapter can be applied to them. Do different approaches fit better for different leaders?
- To what degree do you consider the concept of NPL to give us a better understanding of the leadership challenges in the public sector?
- Discuss the leadership behaviour of the present political leaders. What leadership changes would you like to see happen?
- Picture a leader who in your opinion has a strong ethical and authentic character. What challenges will such a leader experience in the public sector?

Recommended further reading

Bass, M.B. (2008). *The Bass Handbook of Leadership*. New York: Free Press.

Brookes, S. & Grint, K. (2010). "A New Public Leadership Challenge?" in Brookes, S. & Grint, K. (eds) *The New Public Leadership Challenge*. Basingstoke: Palgrave Macmillan, pp. 1–15.

Brown, M.E. & Treviño, L.K. (2006). "Ethical Leadership: A Review and Future Directions," *The Leadership Quarterly*, 17, 595–616.

Gardner, L.G., Cogliser, C.C., Davis, K.M. & Dickens, M.P. (2011). "Authentic Leadership: A Review of the Literature and Research Agenda," *The Leadership Quarterly*, 22, 1120–1145.

Hartley, J. (2010). "Political Leadership," in Brookes, S. & Grint, K. (eds) *The New Public Leadership Challenge*. Basingstoke: Palgrave Macmillan, pp. 133–149.

Yukl, G. (2006). *Leadership in Organizations*. Upper Saddle River, NJ: Pearson Prentice Hall.

Value-based leadership

6

Key learning points

At the end of this chapter the reader should be able to:

- comprehend the theoretical aspects of a theory of leadership based on goal-setting, problem-solving and language creation
- appreciate the way that values develop in leadership and how value-based leadership is embedded in the values of an organization
- realize the importance of the ethical dimension and that value-based leadership should reach throughout an organization
- appreciate the importance of anchoring the leadership process in respect of goal-setting, problem-solving, language, and interaction.

Although value-based leadership as a concept is well established, it lacks a distinct foundation based in leadership theory. Moreover, it is more closely linked to the leader as a person, rather than to the leadership process itself. In order to constitute a meaningful basis for leadership in public professions, value-based leadership should capture the characteristics of professional work. The purpose of this chapter is to define value-based leadership as a process and discuss some theoretical implications.

6.1 Leadership as a process

Although the theories focusing on leadership attributes and leadership styles can be discussed from a perspective of values, they both build a foundation which is inadequate for a model of value-based leadership in professional organizations. They indicate that values are important among both leaders and employees, although it is difficult to take it any further. Focusing primarily on the formal leader is another weakness. A lot of self-leadership is exercised within the professions, and this perspective is difficult to pull into these theories. There is thus a need for a leadership theory which facilitates analysis of the specific challenges associated with professional organizations.

That is why we have decided to choose a process-oriented view of leadership as a starting point, since professionals largely practise self-leadership. This means that all employees to a greater or lesser degree may participate in the leadership process no matter where they are located in an organizational hierarchy. In organizations based on knowledge, where employees have fewer restrictions on their work performance, such a starting point is particularly relevant. This is an important perspective within the theories of shared leadership. This leadership model is defined as an interactive process of influence in small groups where participants lead each other with the aim of realizing the important individual and group goals (Pearce & Conger, 2003). It allows all employees to participate in the leadership process, which largely captures the situation found in professional organizations. It also emphasizes how leadership evolves through active participation and empowerment. Instead of focusing on a formal leader, it is assumed that various leadership functions are distributed among different individuals in a group. Some decisions are made in collaboration while others are made by individual members alone. Although it is an exciting development in this field, we have yet to see a theory that integrates the various research contributions (Yukl, 2006), making shared leadership theory somewhat fragmented.

Some other theories also draw from these perspectives; for example, collective leadership, distributed leadership, and relational leadership (Bolden, Petrov & Gosling, 2009; Friedrich et al., 2009; Uhl-Bien, 2006). A key point here is that leadership is something practised in interaction with others, where the importance of the individual leader is downplayed. Leadership processes can only be understood from the overall interaction between formal leaders and professional workers. Nor do these theories appear in a form that is suitable for developing models for value-based leadership. Therefore, we have chosen a Scandinavian leadership theory which captures many of the same dimensions that are revealed in the theory of shared leadership (Johnsen, 1984, 2002, 2006). Operating within this theoretical genre, Erik Johnsen (2006) defines leadership as *a goal-setting, problem-solving, and language-creating interaction between relevant persons.* This means that all employees may more or less participate in the leadership process, no matter where they are located in an organizational hierarchy. In organizations based on knowledge, where employees have fewer restrictions on their work performance, such a starting point is particularly relevant.

An important perspective in Johnsen's theory is that leadership processes must work at all systemic levels in an organization. Leadership is not something practised by select individuals; it is a necessary function for an organization to exist. The quality of the leadership process is related to its ability to produce rewards for the organization's stakeholders; that is, generate results. Leadership is therefore a necessary function of any organization.

Goal-setting interactions

An important element in this leadership theory is that the definition of leadership is linked to goals, which is common in most leadership definitions. Based on this, leadership is aimed at the continuous development of goals through negotiations and interpretations; hence goals are fashioned out of both conflict and consensus (Barnard, 1938). Leadership is, according to this definition, tied to a process of goal-setting. The goals are divided into three main categories: operational goals, adaptive goals, and development goals.

The operational objectives mean that leaders must constantly have a clear focus on daily operations. Users are entitled to their services, budgets must be held, employees must be paid, and demands from higher authorities must be met. But operational objectives are not sufficient for addressing major changes. In these cases, leaders must find new solutions and work on adaptive goals, possibly resulting in new procedures, new forms of leadership, new services, etc. A college may experience a dramatic drop in the number of applicants, or a hospital may be faced with sizeable cutbacks in funding. If leaders cannot handle the adaptive process, the organization's survival will be at risk. Finally, leaders must work to continuously develop the organization. Services and efficiency must be improved. Employee's expertise must be cultivated, and the organization must be able to cope with future challenges – in other words, development goals are needed in the leadership process.

Problem-solving interactions

The second element in the definition is that leadership is a problem-solving process, which is also common in most leadership definitions. According to Erik Johnsen (2006), the processes of goal-setting and problem-solving will often occur simultaneously. Objectives are adjusted and prioritized while searching for means to achieve the goals. The leadership process thus appears as more complex, and it opens up the possibility of disagreements over both the objectives and means. According to this theory there are three primary ways to solve problems: analysis/synthesis, interaction, and search/learn.

The first way represents a rational process whereby employees who have the necessary expertise engage in analysis to find solutions. This is often not enough, and more people need to be involved. Interaction is especially suitable when the character of the problem affects many people – for example, when implementing organizational changes. The same applies to new problems and problems where there is a need for interdisciplinary expertise. If a satisfactory solution based on the existing skills and knowledge is not possible, a search/learn process must be instigated. Then the organization must learn by testing and failing.

Many situations exist in which all these ways of problem-solving can be used. For leadership to work well, those involved in the leadership processes should have access to a wide range of problem-solving methods, and it is essential to identify which methods are best suited in a given situation.

Language-creating interactions

The last element of the definition is that leadership is a language-creating process. This is a dimension that is rarely found in other definitions of leadership. It is in other words emphasized that those who exercise leadership also must develop a language that makes it possible to work with goal-setting and problem-solving. Here, the language represents the knowledge brought into the leadership process. If a team of teachers at a school is working to create a better classroom environment, they must have knowledge about which dimensions should be stressed (goal-setting), and they need to understand what can be done for making improvements (problem-solving). Therefore, leadership requires knowledge and a relevant conceptual framework for the tasks that are to be solved. The theory differentiates between three languages: decision language, behavioural language, and system language.

Decision language is related to the expertise in the profession and is therefore a dominant language in all professional occupations. This language is used for addressing the specific challenges that arise during the execution of the job. Behavioural language is aimed at understanding human behaviour at an individual, group, or organizational level; for example, an insight into organizational theory, leadership theory, motivational theory, etc. Finally, system language is suitable for understanding the totality of an organization which is necessary when working with the superior and integrated issues in the organization.

A growing understanding of the leadership's communicative function has emerged within the area of leadership; that is, how leaders – through teamwork – formulate the organization's objectives, the importance of a common vision, and the vital role that a common language plays in helping people from different professions understand each other. People with different backgrounds and experiences will often interpret the same event differently. The leadership process will take place among participants with different frameworks of understanding and different perceptions of reality. If it is desirable to create new meanings or new constructions of reality, leadership must have a capacity for action which makes it possible to contribute to a reconstruction of the participants' cognitive structures. Leadership must in other words contribute to a reinterpretation of past events. This may be necessary in order to create a basis for good communication.

Based on this description of the leadership function, leadership emerges as an independent function that must be maintained in any organization. Formal leaders have been given the authority to lead other people; that is, to make decisions that the employees have to follow. However, this is only a small part of what the concept of leadership entails. In today's society it is just as important to lead with others as through others.

There are thus many organizational members who from time to time exert leadership behaviour within an organization. If we sum up this behaviour, we obtain a picture of the complete leadership process in the organization. Based on

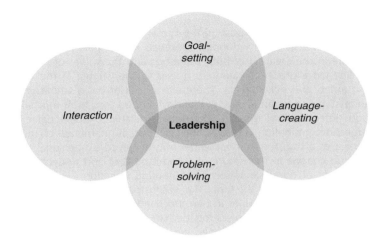

Figure 6.1   Leadership as a goal-setting, problem-solving, and language-creating interaction

this view, we can say that the formal leaders are responsible for the leadership process working in a satisfactory manner within the organization. They are not only responsible for their own leadership behaviour, but they are also responsible for ensuring that all personnel with adequate qualifications participate in the leadership process. They must create an environment where the objectives are held in high esteem and the total expertise is utilized to actively solve problems. A good leader is one who is able to develop a good leadership process within her or his area of responsibility; that is, a leader who has the power to maintain the leadership of the leadership process. This leadership theory is illustrated in Figure 6.1.

6.2   Value-based leadership – a conceptual definition

Based on central conditions from theories on ethical leadership, authentic leadership and transformational leadership, value-based leadership should at least have the following characteristics:

1. Those exercising leadership must have personal values consistent with the values of the organization.
2. Those exercising leadership must have a high ethical standard.
3. Those exercising leadership must be true to their own values.

Example 11

Florence Nightingale

Every year in May a lamp is borne to Westminster Abbey in London to celebrate the role of one leader in creating the nursing profession. Known popularly as the "lady with the lamp" because of her presence on the wards late at night ministering to the sick and wounded, Florence Nightingale is regarded as a critical figure in the creation of both the ethos and the values of professional nursing. She led a group of volunteer nurses to the Crimea in the 1850s to nurse wounded and sick soldiers. There was a lack of basic sanitation and a poor understanding of basic care practice which led to a high mortality rate from both infection and disease. Through leadership by personal example and rugged determination, she was able to effect fundamental change. Her effectiveness as a transformational leader was achieved by personal example and effecting change in the nature of committed care and understanding of the importance of good sanitation in combating infection – something not appreciated by the Army at the time. She was instrumental in embedding both professional and personal values in her effective leadership. Some regard her as a key figure in setting the basis for the National Health Service in the UK. She was an indefatigable campaigner, writing thousands of letters, and was instrumental in effectively utilizing statistics and visual presentation to promote the importance of the cause of both sanitation and professional nursing values.

These theories indicate that the personal characteristics of leaders are the most important variables for explaining value-based leadership. Since professionals have considerable flexibility in their work, it is – as previously mentioned – most convenient to start off with a process-oriented view of leadership. This implies that all employees to a greater or lesser degree may participate in the leadership process, no matter where they are located in an organizational hierarchy. In order to integrate Erik Johnsen's leadership theory with a value-based perspective, we define value-based leadership as:

> Value-based leadership is a goal-setting, problem-solving, language-creating, and value-developing interaction which is anchored in the organization's values and high ethical standards. Value-based leadership can be exercised at the individual level, group level, and organizational level.

Several elements are visible from this definition. For starters, value-based leadership as defined above is linked to a general leadership model (Johnsen, 2006) and can be processed and discussed within all the dimensions associated with this leadership theory. This will ensure that value-based leadership constantly focuses on leadership behaviour; that is, behaviours directed towards achieving key organizational objectives.

Second, the definition points out that value-based leadership should include a value-developing process. This is a central point in transformational leadership, ethical leadership, as well as authentic leadership. Linked with general leadership theory, value development must be integrated with goal-setting, problem-solving, and language-creating. The processes associated with goal-setting must therefore be linked to a discussion about values. Furthermore, the values must actively regulate the problem-solving processes; in other words, values must provide a clear framework for which actions are acceptable. Efforts must also be made to create a language which makes it possible to articulate the organization's prevailing or desired culture. This also implies recognizing the value base's constant state of flux, especially since values enter into political contexts through leadership's connection to fields for conflict and fields for harmony (Johnsen, 2006). This is demonstrated by research showing that the ongoing modernization of the public sector has created increased value-related conflicts (Pollitt, 2003).

Third, and as a key point for transformational leadership, the definition specifies that value-based leadership should be embedded in the organization's values. This means that both leadership and value development must be based on the values that are present. Hence, objectives and problem-solving should be based on fundamental values which are either formalized through a value platform or are inherent in the organizational culture. It also means that the organization must agree on some decisions regarding which are the most important values. If values are too extensive, complex, and conflicting, it will be hard to explicitly pull them into the leadership processes. The organization's values are not necessarily an unambiguous concept, and questions can be asked about which values should serve as the basis for value-based leadership. In this context, such leadership should primarily be based on the values that are dominant in situations where leadership is exercised – that is, in direct leadership interactions. The values in the local environment are therefore central. For a principal and co-workers in a high school, these are the values that are present at the school.

Fourth, the definition specifies that value-based leadership should be founded on high ethical standards, which is a key point in the theories associated with transformational leadership, ethical leadership, and authentic leadership. With reference to ethical leadership, important aspects will be integrity, honesty, trustworthiness, fairness, and caring for both people and society (Treviño et al., 2000). These values can likewise be linked to universal ones that govern the relationship between people. Being universal means they are considered important in all contexts and for all people. Take honesty, for example. There are no situations in which dishonesty is widely acceptable. This is in contrast to some of the other values present in an organization. Loyalty in relation to a superior is in many organizations an important value. However, few people will agree that such loyalty is a universal value which needs to be absolute in all situations.

By linking this to the creation of values, we see that value-based leadership also aims to develop an ethical culture within the organization. This is an important point which separates value-based leadership from leadership processes within organizations or groups which – according to our social norms – are of unethical character; for example, criminal organizations that rest on strong common economic value.

Finally, the definition makes the point that value-based leadership will exist at all levels of the organization. At the individual level, it will be exercised as

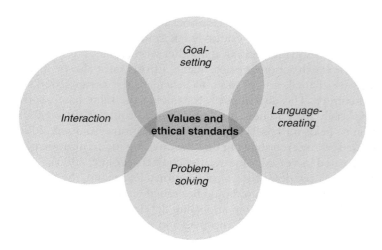

Figure 6.2   Model of value-based leadership

value-based self-leadership, where employees must attach their job behaviour to values, maintain a conscious awareness of the need for creating values, and consciously pursue self-control. This is particularly important in professional occupations where employees have wide latitude. At the group level is team leadership, which will be exercised within close social interactions in tight relationships. At this level, all dimensions within the leadership model are relevant, and the value base must always be present in the performed behaviour. At the organizational level, value-based leadership looks a lot like what is called transformational leadership. The values are also central at this level, and the aim is to create a new image of reality containing new visions and a stronger sense of community. The model is illustrated below in Figure 6.2.

6.3   Basic values of the leadership process

Let us examine what it means when arguing that value-based leadership should have a clear set of values which are anchored both in the organization's values and in high ethical standards. To a certain extent, this represents a dilemma: While the leadership process is based on the organization's values and ethical standards, it is still implicitly assumed that value-based leadership is anchored in the values held by the individual leader – which are essential for authentic leadership. This is illustrated in Figure 6.3.

If we take the definition of value-based leadership, it is desirable to have a strong grounding in the organization's values, in high ethical standards, and in the particular values of the individual leader. The organization's values are tied to the organization's culture or an interpretation of this through a formal value platform. Therefore, these values have an *internal* origin, although the organizational culture also reflects the values of society. Ethical standards are based on ethical norms in the society, and consequently they have an *external* origin.

Figure 6.3 Basic values of the leadership process

They can also be captured in the organization through ethical practices or codes of ethics, although in practice they should conform with society's dominant ethical norms. Finally, the leader's personal values have an individual origin. Each person who participates in the leadership process has his or her own values, and while each is a member of the same organization, variations in values indeed exist at the individual level.

To be a useful concept, value-based leadership should include a larger degree of overlap between these three sets of values. If not, value-related conflicts which can create huge challenges will emerge. An important question is to what extent is it possible to develop consistent values (Bass & Steidlmeier, 1999). Instances where leaders try to transfer their own values to the employees can be regarded as ethical problems, at odds with social-democratic and humanistic values (Stevens et al., 1995), and in conflict with core principles of authentic leadership (Gardner et al., 2011). Therefore, from this perspective, the process of creating values should be subjected to strict requirements. Most notably, the process should be conducted openly so that key values can be discussed by various stakeholders, with the aim of developing a common understanding of what are the organization's most central values.

The leadership theories that explicitly entertain a value perspective all link this to the leader's individual values. When we choose to begin with a process-oriented theory of leadership, the focus shifts from the leader to the leadership process. Thus, we are primarily interested in exploring the value base of the leadership process. Based on our definition, the leadership process consists of a goal-setting, problem-solving, and language-creating interaction. Thus, it is these elements that need a value base, as illustrated in Figure 6.4.

In Figure 6.4, we have firstly illustrated that the leadership process is a holistic one, even though it is divided into four dimensions. Secondly, we have shown that the leadership process must be based on ethical standards. Finally, we have illustrated that the leadership process also must be based on the organization's values.

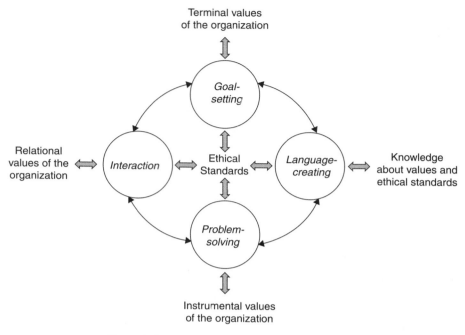

Figure 6.4   Basic values for the leadership process

Assisted dying

There is a range of different approaches to assisted dying in different countries and indeed within countries. In some countries it is permissible for doctors to assist people to die. This may involve prescribing drugs for this express purpose and in some cases it may permit the doctor to actually administer the drug. This difference between countries reflects the differences in the ethical value attached to the preservation of life. It also reflects differences in the values of medical professionals who may accept or refuse a role in assisted dying.

The question of assisted dying is also relevant for instrumental and terminal values. Some view permitting assisted dying as likely to promote pressures on sick and elderly people to avoid becoming a burden on relatives or society. Others argue that the option of assisted dying enables personal choice.

For leaders of healthcare organizations this represents a challenge in both communicating values and also appreciating how values in this area might be changing.

Anchoring the goal-setting process

All organizations have a number of objectives that are somehow included in the leadership process. All these objectives are linked to formal or informal contracts. Using a college as an example, we have a contract between the relevant ministry and the college. This takes the form of an annual grant letter which specifies what the college needs to produce from the allocated budget. These specificities in turn become important overarching goals for the college. The college's board will also formulate other short and long-term requirements for the college's performance, which form the basis of a contract between the board and the principal.

To realize these objectives, the principal will make contracts with the individual departments, which specify how many students will be educated, how much resources will be used, etc. This is passed on to the faculty level, and contracts are established between the faculties and employees. The syllabus represents a contract with each individual student. Behind all these contracts are negotiations and discussions – goal-setting processes. And the objectives can change over time.

A value base for the organization's objectives means that the objectives need to have a solid correlation with the organization's terminal values (Rokeach, 1973). Terminal values represent the end states preferred by a person or a social group. In professional organizations, these goals are important parts of the profession's core values. If the objectives have a solid value base, they will achieve the same "effect" as the values. Moreover, they have both emotional and motivational sides, and this affects the behaviour of the employees. This means that the employees – both managers and regular employees – are committed to achieving the objectives, regardless of formal control systems. It is therefore particularly important to have a solid value base for objectives that are difficult to control in other ways. Examples of such objectives are caring for patients in a hospital or good class environment at a school. However, it is also important to realize that not all objectives of an organization have a solid value base, although this does not mean that the objectives are seen as less important by the employees. Therefore, the organization must have different systems for ensuring that employees give a higher priority to key objectives.

The goals too must be in accordance with high ethical standards. Here, the profession's ethical code is a good starting point. When developing objectives for the operation, they must be compared to a set of ethical rules. In addition to professional ethical guidelines, there are other, more general ethical rules within most organizations. For government employees, a special set of ethical rules are developed.

A major challenge with creating a value base for the objectives is that different values or clusters of values may be in conflict with each other, leading to the formation of negative attitudes among employees towards certain goals, including financial ones. This is not necessarily because financial objectives are viewed as less important, but because strong financial leadership is associated with layoffs and reduced opportunity to work towards other important objectives. The public sector is especially vulnerable to this, where employees to a limited extent can influence the level of organizational budgets.

Anchoring the problem-solving process

In addition to goal-setting, leadership must determine how best to create good results – in other words, how to realize the objectives. Typically, an organization has greater flexibility in choosing their methods than their objectives. This is particularly evident in highly professional government organizations. Politicians establish overall goals and budgets, leaving it up to the subordinate organizations to find necessary methods for achieving the goals.

Naturally, these goals must be adapted to a variety of bureaucratic rules. Some are defined within the law; others are defined in government regulations. Bureaucratic rules may apply to employee rights to participation in various leadership processes, or to formal procedures related to working hours, wages, and other similar issues. Some of these rules cut directly into the leadership process, while others regulate how an organization is managed. However, in principle, the leadership must be given the latitude to make their own decisions. If not, then exercising leadership is pointless.

Anchoring the problem-solving process requires leaders to choose methods that correspond well with the organization's instrumental values. These are practices and professional standards that have a value in terms of status. There is a wide range of professional standards that have developed over time in professional organizations. In addition, there are other patterns of behaviour that over time have developed an intrinsic value. The challenge is to balance good base values with the need to find appropriate solutions. If this becomes problematic, there may need to be an active focus on creating values.

In addition to the instrumental values, the problem-solving process must also be quality-controlled to ensure high ethical standards. Since ethics to a greater extent than objectives regulates behaviour, there are many standards which are relevant for the problem-solving process. We can partially find them under general requirements for ethical character – integrity, honesty, trustworthiness, fairness, and caring – and partially in the general requirements for how decisions should be made. Furthermore, important ethical standards are embedded in ethical rules. For example, the code of ethics for government service applies rules to all employees in state organizations. Finally we can mention the ethical codes that are developed within a profession. These combine to provide a number of ethical rules which should form a solid basis for a value-based, problem-solving process.

Anchoring the language-creating process

Developing efficient leadership processes necessitates common knowledge and conceptual understanding. These must be adapted to the specific challenges and the particular context that exist in the relevant organization. Therefore, the leadership language must to a large extent be created in the local environment where the leadership is exercised. In this context, a value-based anchoring of the language-creating process means a need to develop knowledge about the values and ethical standards among all employees – tailored to the specific tasks to be performed.

This is not just a matter of theoretical knowledge. Values and ethical standards must be grounded in practice; that is, value and ethical reflections must be carried out, where professional workers develop their own language, thus imparting concrete and practical content. For this language to be suitable in a leadership context, it needs to be linked to both goal-setting and problem-solving processes. The managers and employees must therefore be able to discuss which of the terminal values and ethical standards can be used when setting goals. And they must be able to identify which instrumental values and ethical standards should govern problem-solving methods.

Creating language is an underestimated part of the leadership process. And it is especially important in professional organizations, where professional collaboration has always been of great importance. In addition to being a tool, language is also a way to create meaning. By developing greater insights into values and ethical factors, the perceived importance of these factors is transformed. Value dimensions are amplified and appear as central in the leadership process.

Anchoring the interaction process

Based on the applied leadership model, the leadership process will to a large extent be sustained in interaction. However, the processes of interacting can be challenging, especially when the people who will work together have different professional backgrounds, different understanding of the problem's nature, and different ways of thinking. Leadership processes become complex and full of conflicts. This is not necessarily negative, but conflicts need to be managed in ways that minimize the production of adverse side effects.

Using values as an anchor for the interaction process means that interaction is subject to some value and ethical constraints. Both the value platforms and ethical codes within the professions provide good starting points for this. These values are usually aimed at the relations between colleagues, which are also relevant in the context of leadership. Some examples of such values are respect, care, trust, and openness.

6.4   Summary

Organizational leadership is well established as a concept in both practice and in the academic literature. The adoption, expression, and communication of values are a key part of effective leadership, especially in situations involving transformation or change. The chapter takes a process-based view of leadership as a starting point. This is inclusive, implying that all staff participate in leadership is some way. Terms such as collective, distributed, and relational leadership are important in this perspective.

Anchoring the values in respect of goal-setting and the terminal values of the organization is critical. A process which adopts instrumental values inconsistent with the desired end state can raise major ethical concerns. The language used to express values and the interactions between individuals and groups is also critical in Value-based leadership.

Goal-setting and problem-solving are also important elements, and Johnsen avers that they will often occur together. Leadership also involves language and in fact is a language-creating process in itself. Leadership and communication are inextricably linked and language (in whatever form it takes) is at the core. This leads to a four-dimensional model incorporating all these factors.

Value-based leadership derives from theories about ethical, authentic, and transformational leadership. It therefore has characteristics linked to values pertaining to the organization and to the individual. Such values need to be consistent and have an ethical base. Leaders need to be able to display and utilize individual values that have a solid organizational and ethical grounding. Whilst organizational values may vary, there is often a strong societal recognition of values which are viewed positively (such as honesty).

Anchoring the processes of goal-setting, problem-solving, and interaction into value-based leadership is the essence of what needs to be achieved. This anchoring of a value base into leadership is the essence. It is not easy, but once achieved then value-based leadership can be regarded as embedded into the organization, the staff, and the management.

Exercises for further development and understanding

- Identify a leadership challenge in your own organization or from a current public issue (perhaps via a national newspaper story). Using the concepts of goal-setting, problem-solving, and language creation, consider how a leader might respond to this challenge.
- List the values which you as an individual regard as important in how you conduct yourself. Then also list the values which you see as important for society in general and for an organization with which you are familiar. Which values appear on all three lists? Why might there be differences between the lists?
- Sometimes it is argued that the end "justifies" the means used to achieve it. From the perspective of an organizational leader, identify the arguments for and against this proposition.
- Identify how you would communicate key values to different groups of staff within an organization. How might the communication and language be affected by the extent to which the staff are professionals?

- Picture an organization that you are familiar with. Discuss the challenges that might exist with respect to: (a) integrating goals and terminal values; (b) integrating procedures for problem-solving and instrumental values; (c) developing a functional language for discussing value-based leadership; and (d) developing value-based interaction in the leadership processes.

Recommended further reading

Bass, M.B. (2008). *The Bass Handbook of Leadership*. New York: Free Press.

Johnsen, E. (2002). *Managing the Managerial Process: A Participative Approach*. Copenhagen: DJØF Publ.

Leadership and value development

7

Key learning points

At the end of this chapter the reader should be able to:

- appreciate that individual values are established through upbringing and socialization, whereas organizational values are in greater flux
- understand how learning will affect value acquisition utilizing learning theory to assist in this
- recognize the importance of motivation theories in understanding the dimensions of values
- understand how emotion will affect value acquisition and expression
- understand the reflective processes in dealing with values and ethical conflicts.

The values of an organization are to some extent always in motion. This is especially true for values which are less fundamental and can change through practice. Moreover, the entrance of new employees can stimulate discussions on how the job should be conducted. New opinions can be created and the values can be adjusted accordingly. While less abrupt, perhaps, societal values also change from one generation to the next. It is also important to be aware that the values of the individuals are stable over time (Meglino & Ravlin, 1998). An important reason is that they are created through socialization processes and taught in an absolute manner (Rokeach, 1976). It is always either/or. Values related to honesty, caring, respect, and democracy are created through strong socialization processes in which individuals are integrated into a social group. They are part of a common identity and are therefore hard to change.

7.1   Change of values

Those working with value-based leadership must always be open to adjustments of the fundamental values. We must at the same time be aware that our values are an important part of our identity – both as a person and as a professional practitioner. Value transformation is therefore a challenging task, and we can ask whether it is possible in practice. As previously pointed out, this also has an ethical aspect (Stevens et al., 1995). Is it ethically acceptable to implement processes aimed at changing employees' personal values?

It must be emphasized that value development is not necessarily about replacing "unsuitable" values with more "functional" values. It is more appropriate to talk about a realignment of values, where some values acquire centrality while others lose it. As shown in Chapter 4, it can be argued that values are organized in a hierarchy (Hodgkinson, 1996): rather than some values replacing others, values move between different levels by losing or gaining status and importance. An example of this is found in a Norwegian study (Busch & Wennes, 2012) which shows that in a Norwegian municipality, the values of equality, continuity, and responsibility have decreased in importance over the last ten years, while user orientation, innovation, and professional standards have increased. Thus, value development had occurred without any of the values being replaced.

Another possibility is to make adjustments to the cognitive, emotional, or motivational dimensions of key values. Cognitively speaking, values will become evident by being inserted into the language and pulled into our daily conversations. A value can therefore become increasingly important when given a stronger focus in the organization. A similar process unfolds when a value is imbued with a new interpretation. Although we have many values in society, they are often interpreted differently by different people. If we ask ten nurses to describe the concept of altruism, we will most likely be faced with several different answers. If we compare the answers with the definition found in a dictionary, we may find that no-one has the "correct" definition. This is true for most concepts. The cognitive content of a value is developed through social processes by which each individual creates his own subjective interpretation.

This allows for the possibility of values always being interpretable in new ways. For example, in the police we find the value "force loyalty." This is an important value in professions where employees regularly confront threatening situations and must be able to rely on each other as a result. While force loyalty specifies that the members of a group must have strong loyalty to each other, it can at the same time lead to a reluctance to report or prosecute unethical behaviour. If this happens, it may be necessary to re-interpret the value in order to retain its positive features and reduce its negative ones, which is not necessarily an easy process. There may be battles about interpretations, and leaders do not necessarily have more influence than others (Czarniawska, 2000).

Value development may also include changing the emotional and motivational dimensions of a value. For example, in a school it may be necessary to emphasize respect as a way to deal with feelings of being bullied. In cases like this, it will not be sufficient to simply make the value respect more visible, although it may be an important first step. To make an emotional change towards the value, it may be necessary to display what happens to those who are bullied. This can create sympathy which in turn enhances the emotional dimension, as employees become angry or upset if they hear or observe bullying at school. To enhance the motivation, teachers can be trained in how to deal with bullying issues and how to deal with difficult students. This way, one of the existing values can obtain a new emotional and motivational content.

7.2   Value development through learning

Learning is an important prerequisite for value development – both at the individual and at the organizational level. When a child is socialized, she or he will acquire the basic values of society. And when we become educated or acquire a job, we will learn the predominant values within the communities we join. During the early stages of life, we primarily learn basic values like confidence, honesty, kindness, and caring. As we grow up, we learn more complex values like integrity, justice, equality, and democracy. Previously we have demonstrated that the concept of value has cognitive, motivational, and emotional dimensions, and the learning process must capture all of these aspects. When we learn that honesty is important, we learn the meaning of the term, we become motivated to act with honesty, and we develop an emotional response to experiencing excessive honesty or dishonesty. Learning theory is a complex discipline, and we have no intention of providing a detailed introduction to the field in this book. However, to gain greater insight into the challenges of value development, we will take a closer look at some learning aspects related to the three concepts of cognition, motivation, and emotion.

Cognitive learning

Cognitive learning is related to the mental processes that govern the creation, organization, and retrieval of knowledge. Knowledge is not stored as individual pieces, but exists as structures where the individual parts are integrated with each other. This interconnected structure consists of a number of cognitive maps being recalled when we encounter a new situation. When a child welfare consultant meets a troubled family for the first time, he or she will get a number of impressions of the parents, the children, and the home (mood, emotions, body language, verbal expressions, physical conditions, etc.). The consultant will then bring up a cognitive schema (developed through education and past experience) which places all the information into a meaningful context. A special type schema called *a script* indicates what type of behaviour is appropriate in a given situation. This means that the child welfare consultant also knows what to do in the current situation.

If the situation suddenly changes – for example, if one of the parents becomes aggressive – the script adjusts to fit the new situation and specifies how the consultant should handle this. An experienced professional practitioner has thousands of scripts like this. Based on cognitive learning theory, we can say that what characterizes experienced employees is their knowledge about many cognitive scripts that relate to the job. Beginners have far fewer scripts and are therefore more likely to be incapable of action in a new situation. They do not realize what is going on and have no script that provides instructions on how they ought to act.

Cognitive learning theory stresses that learning occurs through active reflection related to our own experiences. New knowledge is created in an active process where we challenge our own knowledge, develop new and more advanced cognitive maps, and adjust our own behaviour (Kolb et al., 1995). We learn through our own experiences and by observing others. The latter is called model learning and has proven to be an effective form of learning (Bandura, 1986). Model learning is central to professional careers. Since novices learn by observing the behaviour of experienced colleagues, they do not need to directly experience all that has been done before them, thus allowing for the avoidance of past mistakes. They learn the appropriate way immediately by replicating the behaviour of others. In addition to observing the behaviour, it is even possible to observe cognitive reasoning. An experienced worker can, for example, describe how a specific job should be carried out, and share her reflections on the challenges associated with this. Research has demonstrated that this supports the process of transferring new knowledge to one's own work situation (Harmon & Evans, 1984).

Using cognitive theory for value development means that the values have to be inserted into the language. We need to develop a conceptual framework that makes it possible to discuss values like altruism, caring, respect, justice, equality, etc. Firstly the values need to have a meaningful content. Employees should be able to describe the contents of the values, and a common understanding of the values should be developed through the leadership process. Secondly, a cognitive structure where the various values are placed in relation with each other must be developed. Are values organized into clusters? Are there any values that are more important than others? Finally, appropriate scripts need to be developed; that is, knowledge indicating the behaviour which is required if one is to act in accordance with the values. What does it mean in practice to treat colleagues with respect? What procedures must be followed in order to achieve fairness? How do we take care of our own integrity?

A major challenge in cognitive learning is related to what we call *theories-in-use* and *espoused theories* (Argyris & Schön, 1978). Theories-in-use represents the knowledge (scripts) which effectively governs our behaviour. This knowledge can exist on a subconscious level – in other words, it is tacit. Espoused theories, by contrast, consist of the knowledge we claim to base our actions on – in other words, they are explicit. It is possible to develop advanced cognitive maps of the organization's values and how these should be complied with (espoused theories) without this having any practical consequences. For example, systematic training on how teachers should identify and handle problems with bullying could be implemented without anyone doing anything about it in practice. We can call this a difference between theory and practice. Therefore, we risk implementing a programme for developing values which only ends up in a change of the espoused theories, while the theories-in-use remain untouched. In such a case, learning will have had no impact on organizational action, and in many ways be worthless in an organizational context. Expressing to oneself and to others that one wants change and development is of little use if one continues to act the same way as before.

Another challenge may be linked to what Argyris & Schön (1978) refer to as single-loop learning and double-loop learning. *Single-loop learning* means that one does not question the fundamental values that are established in an organization. One may become more adept at doing the job, but remain unable to find less conventional solutions. At a university, there may, for example, be strong values tied to engaging in lecturing. The quality of the lectures can be improved upon through evaluations and discussions. However, this is not a solution if there is a need for more extensive changes like introducing entirely new forms of learning. In order to be able to challenge fundamental values, which are often grounded in theories-in-use, one needs to engage in *double-loop learning*. This is far more demanding, and the organization needs to critically identify and focus on established truths. Although the aforementioned university has teaching quality as a central value, it will not through single-loop learning have the power to identify its values-in-use. The opportunity to find a more appropriate behaviour to achieve key values is thereby being blocked.

So-called tacit knowledge (Nonaka & Takeuchi, 1995) is generally a challenge in cognitive learning. This is a form of knowledge that is difficult to express in words since we are not able to immediately articulate it. We cannot process it by using language, which makes it challenging to render a clear understanding of our own knowledge. Tacit knowledge often occurs when we expand our skills. We learn a new behaviour without necessarily putting it into words. An example of this is how patients are cared for in a hospital. Nurses respond to patients' needs and treat them individually without necessarily reflecting on their own behaviour. Comfort, encouragement, body contact, and care are provided without the nurses reflecting upon what to do. This knowledge is developed through practice and guidance from knowledgeable colleagues. You know you have it, you know how to use it in practice, but you do not quite know how to articulate it.

Example 13

Lausanne Police

An award-winning example of values change through education was shown by the Lausanne Police in Switzerland. The police often have a quite inward-looking culture which leads to defensiveness and values resistant to criticism.

In Lausanne this led to an initiative whereby formal ethical education was introduced for police officers. The change was not easy to introduce as it had to confront the traditional police culture. The initiative sought to develop in police officers a reflective ability based upon formal, academic, ethical training. This was associated with a charter setting out key values. It impacted positively on the problem-solving of the police. Leadership was a critical factor in gaining acceptance and commitment to a new set of values.

Developing motivation

One of the main reasons for values having behavioural consequences is the fact that values have a motivational dimension. During the process of developing values, it is therefore very important to have a focus on this dimension as well. Motivation is an expression of a person's needs, desires, interests, and internal focus. It can as a consequence explain why we invest more energy in some tasks and less in others. Although a variety of theories exists on the concept of motivation, it is still a complex phenomenon. People are different and have different needs, which will change with age, life situations, and social expectations. There are therefore no theories that can predict what will motivate a particular person (Schein, 1978). We will take a closer look at needs theories and cognitive theories, since we believe they are best suited for discussing motivation in relation to values.

The most notable needs theory was developed by Abraham Maslow (1954), who distinguished between six different needs according to their position in a hierarchy. This theory has been further developed by Alderfer (1972), who drew a distinction between three need types:

1. Existence (physiological and safety needs)
2. Relatedness (the desire for social relations and good interpersonal relationships)
3. Growth (needs for recognition, growth, and personal development).

In what is sometimes referred to as ERG theory (existence, relatedness, growth), motivation is created by individuals seeking to meet their needs. The particular need that dominates will vary from situation to situation and from person to person. Needs may also be latent and activated in special circumstances. The question relevant in the context of value-based leadership is whether there is any link between values that we want to amplify and these categories of needs. This is especially relevant with the last two – relatedness and growth.

If we begin with the core values of the professions, we will see that there are many values which have a social dimension; for example, caring, altruism, participation, respect, and user orientation. Focusing on these types of values can activate relational needs and thus link them to a motivational dimension. The value caring motivates because it touches some deep human need. When working with these types of values, it may be important to tie them to a social and relational dimension.

The growth needs indicate the necessity of doing a good job, learning, and continuing to develop and exploit our potential. In addition, they capture the need for esteem and social status. Firstly means that values with a high status in the organization can create motivation. If it is desirable to promote certain values, these ought to be placed at the centre. Motivation can be boosted by rewarding employees who, in words and action, show that they give high priority to certain values. In addition, values which are difficult to obtain can activate a need for personal development. For example, at a school that has scored low on national tests, it may be desirable to place greater emphasis on the objective value of "savvy students." A motivation linked to this value may be based on a growth need. To increase the level of knowledge among the students, it may be necessary to implement new teaching methods or establish new forms of collaboration between teachers. This may require teachers to challenge themselves and try new paths. They are, in other words, given an opportunity for personal growth.

The weakness with the needs theories is that they do not problematize the choice of actions. There is little value added if one is highly motivated to improve the skills and knowledge of students but does not know how to put this desire into action. Theories of cognitive motivation include this aspect. They assume that when a need is activated, two questions will be asked (Porter & Lawler, 1968; Vroom, 1964):

1. What is the probability that a given action leads to the desired result?
2. What reward does this give me?

If it is not possible to find a satisfactory action, motivation will decrease. An active need then does not lead to a consequence. However, if there is a solution which in addition provides a personal reward, the motivation will be reinforced. The reward can be, for example, the feeling of good achievement (intrinsic reward) or praise from colleagues (external reward).

These theories show that the motivation generated by activating the needs can be reduced through a subjective analysis of the possible actions, possible consequences, and possible rewards. We can, based on this, draw the conclusion that it is not enough to learn that a value is important. Employees must also learn how to live by the value and see what rewards this brings.

In the previous chapter, we mentioned that model learning is an important form of learning (Bandura, 1986). In addition to showing important principles of cognitive learning, this learning theory sets the focus on two other factors – namely skills and self-efficacy. The emphasis on skills recognizes that knowledge on its own is not enough to create new behaviours. Employees must also develop necessary skills – they need to carry out their actions in practice. Developing skills may therefore be necessary to ensure that values influence employee behaviour.

Self-efficacy is a form of professional self-esteem, or our confidence that we are able to perform or master a specific task. This form of efficacy can be high in one area and low in another. For example, a child-welfare consultant is highly efficacious when it comes to dealing with disadvantaged families, and marginally efficacious when dealing with families with high economic and social status. Self-efficacy is of great importance in determining to what extent we convert our knowledge into practice. Low self-efficacy may act as an obstacle to motivation. Self-efficacy will firstly affect the selection of actions insofar as we choose those actions which we master confidently. Secondly, it affects the level of ambition in the goals we set. Individuals with low self-efficacy, as opposed to high self-efficacy, tend to set unambitious objectives. Thirdly, self-efficacy has an impact on how much effort we put into conducting a task. People with high self-efficacy would place more energy into reaching the objectives. Finally, self-efficacy affects endurance. People with high self-efficacy do not give up so easily when they encounter problems, but try to endure until they have the forces to perform the task.

This means that in order to ensure robust motivation with regard to key values, high self-efficacy must be developed in relation to securing the implementation of necessary actions. Knowledge and skills are not enough by themselves. Employees must also have faith in their abilities to put procedures into practice, with good results. High self-efficacy is best developed by providing employees with challenges that are appropriate to their level of competence.

Emotions and learning

Emotions are also a key element in the concept of values. At the same time, there is currently a consensus that emotional development is shaped by a combination of nature and nurture. This indicates that changing the emotional nature of values is more challenging than simply changing cognitive maps and motivation. Some of the main categories of emotions are joy, love, anger, fear, sadness, and surprise (Greenberg, 2002). Within these groups are a number of more specific emotions. Anger, for example, has different forms, such as disgust, jealousy, rage, and irritation. Emotions can also be divided according to whether they are perceived as negative or positive – in other words, whether they are experienced as pleasant or unpleasant. Furthermore, the strength of the emotion may vary. On the negative side, it can fluctuate between a mild irritation and intense rage. On the positive side, we have variations between some indefinable happiness to elated joy.

Emotional life grows from childhood to adulthood. It gains complexity over time, and we are able to distinguish between several sensations. We will also develop the ability to control our emotions so that they do not create problems for ourselves and others. The learning-related part of this is that emotion is linked to events, situations, and various objects – including values. Some people experience positive emotions when they exercise while others associate it with negative experiences. All these are learned responses that are unique to the individual or to certain social groups. It is this form of learning that is interesting in terms of value development.

A great deal of this learning can be classified as *learning by conditioning*. This is a form of learning that occurs automatically and without any conscious reflection. The principal mechanism is that a given event or object produces a certain feeling. Let us assume that two parents are playing with their children in a relaxed atmosphere without any conflicts. This creates a feeling of happiness among all the participants: They are happy together. Whenever this situation occurs, these feelings are activated. The next step is to assume that this family plays a certain song or melody every time they experience this form of interaction. Learning by conditioning means that the good feelings generated by playing with the children are now being transferred to the melody. If they later hear this melody in a completely different context, the same sense of happiness occurs. Many people find that a certain song or a certain smell brings out "old" feelings which are products of conditioning that took place earlier in life.

This also applies to values. For example, a country's national day, which might be associated with democracy and freedom, can for most people be an emotional experience associated with positive feelings. This creates a learning process where these values have an emotional component insofar as they are associated with the same positive feelings which are also linked to national day. This is reinforced by the fact that democracy, or the lack thereof, in other situations is presented in an emotional context, as seen in a dramatic documentary about a war or news stories about major assaults against people living under dictatorships.

Parallel to connecting events with emotions, a form of *generalization* is taking place. We can say that the emotions are spilling over into nearby concepts. If a strong, positive feeling for democracy is developed, this connector can eventually include values such as equality, fairness, transparency, and freedom of expression. Thus, the positive emotions for a value can be transmitted through generalization to nearby values. Another important concept is *discrimination*, which means that emotions are only transmitted to a limited set of nearby values. For example, the positive feelings towards democracy are only transferred to other specific values – in other words, not all values can be linked to democracy as a form of government.

The majority of the advertisements we encounter in society are based on this form of learning. When we, at the beginning of a major sporting event on TV, are presented with the name of the TV sponsors, the aim has been for us to transfer the strong emotional experiences of watching a football match or an athletic event to the sponsors and their products. A similar process unfolds when we watch a Coca-Cola commercial that presents young people bursting with joy and zest for life. The positive feelings generated by watching these spirited youngsters are expected to be transferred to the cola product. And research shows that it works, even if we do not like being affected by advertising. Learning happens automatically.

It is important to note that this form of learning can also break the link between an event and an emotion, where the value can lose its emotional component. Thus the value can lose much of its capacity to regulate behaviour. Let us assume that user orientation is a strong value in a particular professional organization. If employees within the organization have highly negative emotions associated with users, the positive feelings for user orientation may deteriorate. The basis for the negative emotions may be that some users act in ways that make the employee uncomfortable, or it is hard to satisfy the user's needs for a variety of reasons. Employees will experience negative emotions, and this can automatically be transferred to users as a group. A positive emotional dimension associated with user orientation can then weaken or even be replaced by negative emotions.

We can then raise the question of whether or not this form of learning can work on value development. The answer is obviously yes. First, generalization can be emphasized. "New" values can consciously be linked to existing values that have a strong emotional basis. An effort can be made, through discussion and reflection, to demonstrate that the new value is captured by another more general value. In a hospital it may, for example, be desirable for physicians to put more emphasis into "seeing" the whole patient instead of just focusing on the patient's disease. Since altruism is a strong value in the medical profession, a stronger holistic perspective of the patient can be inserted into a perspective of altruism. The positive emotions of altruism may be transferred over to the "new" value that it is desirable to amplify.

It is also possible to reinforce emotions by pulling values into a situation characterized by positive feelings. Such situations are plentiful. They can, for example, occur when employees receive positive feedback, when they have solved a difficult problem, when major events are celebrated, or when they receive positive coverage in the media. If values are introduced in situations like this, learning by conditioning may occur. The positive emotions of the situation are transferred to these values, which must be made visible and introduced in stories that tie the values to the current situation.

Another question is whether this is ethically correct to do. Even though the intentions are good, it may be interpreted as manipulation (Stevens et al., 1995). When learning is so automatic, employees lose the ability to decide whether or not they want to adjust their values. We have previously specified that value-based leadership must be built on high ethical standards. Conscious efforts to change the emotional basis of employees' values quickly fall into a grey area. Despite this, it is important to have insights into how emotions develop in an organization, both to discern hidden strategies and to better analyse the value development processes.

7.3   Value development through reflection

In the previous section, we have shown that there can be major challenges linked to learning and changing behaviour. It is not sufficient to learn *about* new values. Rather, the individual must search deeper within herself to identify her own values and gain a better connection to her own behaviour. A conscious reflection in this context proves to be a fruitful method, especially in terms of ethical issues. Reflection is a method in which our own thoughts are inserted into a larger contemporary perspective. Connections are made between past and present experiences in order to develop more complex cognitive maps. We shall insert our challenges into new perspectives, develop new interpretations, and then adjust our own behaviours accordingly (Hatton & Smith, 1995). It is also important to view challenges in a historical and cultural perspective.

In what follows, we will present a concrete model of reflection designed to work with ethical dilemmas (Aadland, 2011; Eide & Aadland, 2008). The model has four phases:

1. Problem owner's preconceptions
2. Analysis of the situation
3. Action alternatives
4. Action.

These four phases point to the necessity of starting with a deep analysis of our own personal base before focusing on the specific situation and how a dilemma can be handled in practice. This is illustrated in Figure 7.1.

Problem owner's preconceptions

Preconception is defined as our prior understanding; that is, the background for the way we understand a situation. It is often unconscious and requires a

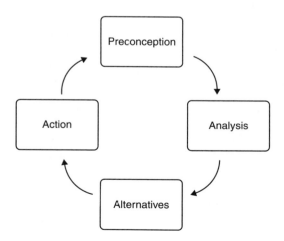

Figure 7.1   Value development in a reflection process

great deal of self-awareness to see our own understanding in a larger perspective. This may be the most difficult phase of a reflection process. Let us assume that a young high-school teacher in his first meeting with the class observes several students sitting immersed in their personal computer. The teacher assumes they are on Facebook and threatens to take action against the students. The students protest, claiming they were merely browsing a relevant academic site. It all ends in a confrontation and a bad start for the teacher. In retrospect, the teacher wonders why it ended the way it did. Why did he assume they were on Facebook? Why was he provoked by the protests? Why was he so annoyed at the time? The explanation may lie in an unconscious interpretation of the situation and an unconscious pattern of behaviour, which is part of the teacher's preconception. If this particular teacher wishes to change his behaviour and handle situations like this more constructively, it will first be necessary to be aware of the underlying thoughts that govern his action.

In ethical reflection, the first step is to identify the core of the situation which created the challenges. The best solution is if reflection can address one central dilemma and two alternative courses of action. In addition, a list should be made of all the individuals present in the situation or affected by the chosen action. Ethical reflection should therefore start with clarifying and reforming the practice that has created an ethical dilemma or conflict.

Let us stick to the teaching profession. A teacher has, for example, a problem with an 18-year-old student who is in his third year in high school. The student has been absent a lot, and there is suspicion of substance-abuse problems. He is disruptive when present and in conflict with both teachers and classmates. The parents have contacted the school several times. However, without the student's consent (he has turned 18), the teachers are not allowed to keep the parents informed. There is no doubt that the student needs help, but he refuses to accept it from the school. The situation is complex and serious, and in order to simplify the situation, the teacher can choose to focus on one question: Should parents be informed or not? This situation affects many people: students, parents, teachers, colleagues, the principal of the school, and officials in the county administration. This situation contains only two solutions.

However, it is not enough just to clarify the situation. It is also necessary to reflect on what values are being challenged. This type of analysis provides greater awareness of the person's preconception. A simple methodology is recommended here, starting with setting up a list which shows the positive reasons for both solutions. This can provide a thorough overview of which values are involved. In order to facilitate this task, it can be based on the profession's values or ethical standards. The analysis will probably reveal that key values can be used as arguments for both actions.

In a process of reflection, it is important to have several persons involved. These may be colleagues who jointly have the same experiences, or people who have experience conducting reflection processes. This is particularly important when it comes time to move a step further and identify more concealed values that may be present in the situation. At this point we need to be challenged by others; it is after all not easy to identify our own preconceptions. We need to drill deeper and search for values outside the profession's core ones.

Analysis of the situation

This is the second phase of the reflection process, as identified in Figure 7.1 above. A more fundamental analysis of the identified dilemma is conducted in this phase. It will be of great help if similar ethical dilemmas are identified earlier. A search on the internet can, for example, reveal that a great deal is written about the ethical dilemmas that may arise when students at high school turn 18. While this fundamental analysis cannot substitute for an analysis of one's own preconceptions, it can serve as a way to gain adequate knowledge from background material.

In this phase, the primary objective of the analysis is to develop greater insight into the ethical dilemma identified. To do so requires greater knowledge about ethical theories – whether virtue ethics, deontological ethics, or proximity ethics. The theories make it easier to see the fundamental aspects of the situation, while also contributing to the development of a more precise language.

If challenges are created by a more general value-problem, it may then be relevant to consider the theories about the concept of value. You can then discuss the cognitive, motivational, and emotional dimension of the values involved. The organization of the values should also be considered, along with potential conflicts between different values and the effect these conflicts might have on employee behaviour. In this process, one's practices and preconceptions are integrated with a more fundamental analysis. We will thus achieve a different and more solid form of learning and a more solid foundation for behavioural change.

Alternatives for action

In this third phase, it is desirable to identify alternatives for action. Due to the strong ties to practices, those involved have probably seen several opportunities for action from the previous two phases. Now these options must be put on the table, evaluated, and weighed against each other. This means that possible consequences must be evaluated, where the challenge is to find the alternative that causes the least harm to those who will be affected. This is no small task: one characteristic of an ethical dilemma is that there are no alternatives that lack negative consequences.

In our school example, one alternative would be for the teacher to contact the parents privately and give them confidential information. Another option would be for the school authorities to inform the police about their suspicion of illegal drug use at school. A third option would involve the teacher putting more pressure on the student to initiate a meeting with the school counsellor. By listing the possible options and at the same time analysing their potential consequences, the problem owner will achieve a better foundation for choosing what should be done.

Action

The last phase is to select one of the possible solutions and put it into practice. This phase must be executed effectively, since it is crucial and can potentially have a major impact on the result. It is also essential to evaluate what happens. No matter how detailed the analysis, it is not possible to anticipate all possible effects. This phase is therefore also a learning process. If things go wrong, you have to try to figure out what happened and make a better decision the next time the same dilemma arises.

7.4   Model for cultural development

It is a greater challenge to change several values in an organization, as it may entail altering essential elements of the professional culture. We will now take a closer look at a model that can be used in situations where more than one organizational value needs to be transformed (Schein, 2010). According to this model, a transformation process can be described in three phases – unfreeze, change, and refreeze (Lewin, 1951). The purpose of unfreezing is for the employees to recognize the need for behavioural changes. The change phase is for establishing a more appropriate form of behaviour, while this behaviour is consolidated in the last phase. In other words, the behaviour should to a certain degree be automated. New behaviour should be performed by employees like a reflex, without having to think about what to do.

Unfreezing phase

In the unfreezing phase, the aim is to destabilize the organization and show that the existing culture has dysfunctional aspects. The employees have to realize that a severe incompetence is present in the organization. In this phase they have to move from an unconscious incompetence to a conscious incompetence. This can be done either through a negative focus or through a positive focus.

With a *negative focus*, the aim is to provide information that arouses unpleasant feelings (Schein, 2010). It is, at the same time, important to develop enough confidence so that the employees are open to learning. Let us look at an example from a hospital. In many countries, there is criticism about dying elderly patients not receiving adequate care in their final hours. This does not apply to pain management, but more towards the patients receiving sufficient nutrition and care. Part of the explanation may lay in the organizational culture, in which the value "care" is only weakly linked to these types of patient situations. Furthermore, there is the possibility that doctors and nurses have developed behaviours where they – without any special reflection – leave these patients to their relatives. This can be characterized as a dysfunctional part of the culture that affects a particular group of patients.

A negative focus entails the doctors and nurses affected being informed that these patients experience strong discomfort during the final days before they die. This creates a sense of guilt and bad conscience, which again provides a solid basis for implementing a change. In order not to cause resistance, conflicts, and denials of responsibility, those involved must be given some psychological safety which allows for learning. They need to feel confident that no one is looking for scapegoats.

A *positive focus* means that doctors and nurses are involved in a process where they get to discuss their professional values in relation to various patient situations, including elderly patients who are dying. The question to be asked is whether their behaviour is consistent with their values. Doctors and nurses can then, through reflection, come to the conclusion that it is advisable to change behaviour. They have realized that they, over time, have developed a pattern of behaviour that is not in line with their fundamental professional values.

In this process, a challenge can occur when employees develop so-called defensive routines (Argyris, 2001). In other words, unconscious strategies have been developed in order to avoid issues that create unpleasant emotions. Every organization has topics that are never up for debate. Perhaps the topics create anxiety, aggression, shame, or other negative emotions that employees are unable to handle. This results in the production of strategies or defensive routines for avoiding those unpleasant situations, but it also results in obstructions to learning.

It is a big problem if these "unquestionable" topics are related to inappropriate behaviours. Dysfunctional behaviours can then be maintained over a longer period of time. As an example, we can assume that student surveys sometimes reveal that students can be bullied by their teachers. We will not take a position on whether this is correct – these surveys may have some methodological weaknesses. However, even if a teacher is bullying students, it may still be an issue that is unquestionable. If it is brought up, it will be rejected, or the surveys will be dubbed as unreliable. This can happen despite the fact that many colleagues might know that a fellow teacher is mistreating some of the students. A defensive routine has been aroused, making it difficult or impossible to address the issue.

Many challenges are tied to an attempt to change the culture around defensive routines. The subject cannot be discussed, and thus it becomes impossible to create unpleasant feelings around the subject. A positive focus is blocked in the same way. This becomes especially difficult if the formal leaders are likewise captured by the culture. They will then never openly acknowledge the problem, and they will never involve the particular issue in a process of change. In situations like this, it may be necessary to bring in external assistance, which may challenge the internal culture and implement the necessary learning processes.

Change phase

A behavioural change can occur automatically after the unfreezing phase. When employees recognize, both cognitively and emotionally, that they have developed a dysfunctional behaviour, it may create an immediate behavioural change. If doctors and nurses develop a feeling of guilt for not providing adequate care for dying patients, their actions can change quickly. Here, the emotional component is essential. Emotions provide energy (Izard, 1992) and create a strong drive for change, especially if the feelings are shared and cultivated in a social community (Collins, 1990). Then the interaction itself will create new energy.

Therefore, in this phase we will move from conscious incompetence to conscious competence. A process will be instigated, aimed at establishing a new behaviour. This is a cognitive process deliberately seeking a more appropriate behaviour. The focus is more on changing actions rather than changing the values. The reason for this is that the behaviour is more visible and is easier to influence. We can also say that the behaviour is more important than the underlying values. Not all employees may change their values during a process like this. But they will adapt to the dominant values in their environments. To put it bluntly, it is more important that a nurse provides a dying patient with adequate care than it is that this action is in line with his or hers own values.

Refreezing phase

In this phase we will move from conscious competence to unconscious competence. It is in other words desirable to automate new behaviours and new values. In the example from the hospital, dying patients should receive good care without the doctors or nurses considering what they are doing. It should be a natural part of how they conduct their professional work. Without changes reaching this stage, relapses can arise swiftly. The moment we release the focus from the new changes, it is very easy to fall back into old habits.

It is important to document that the new behaviour provides better results (Schein, 2010). If doctors and nurses receive praise from relatives for the care they give, or see for themselves that patients have it better, the behaviour is reinforced. In order to automate the behaviour, it must become a habit. However, it is also important to check and make sure the organization is on the right track and doesn't fall back into old habits. There is always a reason why unfortunate habits have evolved in an organization. At a hospital, time pressure and lack of resources can press for a reduced prioritization of some patients, despite being central values. If the underlying causes for unfortunate habits are not addressed, it is easy to unconsciously revert to previous behaviour during the consolidation phase.

7.5   Dealing with conflicting values

Although it is important to work with the transformation of an organization's values, one must normally accept that value conflicts are part of the everyday life in most organizations. These conflicts must be dealt with in the leadership process. This includes value-based leadership. This is not necessarily negative. Conflicting values can also positively impact the organization. Employees must argue for their own values, which can stimulate learning and create a greater consciousness around values. It can also inspire greater attention to the link between values and behaviours. Arguing that a value is of importance is not good enough; the value must also be a guide for one's own behaviour. To keep the value debate alive, it is an advantage to have different values present. This creates tension that leads to greater awareness of both one's own values and behaviours.

We must, at the same time, recognize that having a variety of different values is a challenge to the leadership process. This is best observed in situations where several professions are represented. At a hospital, doctors, nurses, psychologists, physiotherapists, and many other types of health professions are present, in addition to large groups of employees without a healthcare background. Economists, lawyers, and engineers can all create their own subcultures with distinct values that are cultivated through education and practice. Most public institutions have various arrays of subcultures. There can be significant differences in the values established within these groups, which can create difficult value conflicts. Leadership processes must therefore also function in situations containing conflicting values.

Value conflicts do not mean that value-based leadership will not work; it simply means that more time must be allocated to discussing the values that are present. Leaders must work in areas characterized by both harmony and conflict. If conflict dominates, a greater insight into how to handle conflicts is required. Respect for each other's values must be developed, and employees must be able to control negative emotions. When value differences surface, it may be beneficial to focus on the cognitive dimension. What are the differences, how large are they, and how important are they for the decisions that are to be made? A thorough analysis of the values may be enough to make them workable in the leadership process. Differences in values do not necessarily obstruct good solutions.

Research results support this. A research project looked into how organizations handle different logics, a process which for the most part is the same as dealing with different sets of values (Fjellvær, 2010). This particular project found three ways to integrate different logics/values:

1. Dominant mode of integrating logics
2. Balancing mode of integrating logics
3. Cycling mode of integrating logics.

The first method means that leaders select one value system as the dominant one. These values are then given highest priority in situations containing value conflicts. In child welfare, for example, the professional values may be the ones given the most emphasis. If conflicts in relation to economic or bureaucratic values arise, the professional child-welfare values come first.

The second method is more demanding, and acknowledges that reality is often complex and the solutions are rarely straightforward. Based on the given situation or the tasks that need to be completed, the leaders have to prioritize key values. The organization must possess an adequate capacity for conflict resolution and an awareness of what values are present. In child welfare, they may, based on an overall assessment, choose to streamline their operations, although this may degrade the quality of the service.

The final model tries to organize the decision-making situations so that value conflicts do not surface. The problems are treated sequentially and are separated from each other. Taking our child-welfare organization example, this means that a decision on streamlining operations does not consider the possible effects on the quality of service. And no financial implications are assessed when deciding to change academic standards.

When it comes to dealing with value conflicts in practice, the same research shows that many leaders are committed to building strong relations between different groups and individuals. When diverse groups – each with their own values – gain a sense of familiarity with one another, a certain level of mutual tolerance and respect materializes. Thus, it will be easier to keep negative emotions in check and accept the inclusion of each other's values in the leadership process. We might say that this strategy has an emotional focus. When people get to know each other, they will develop positive feelings for each other, and these feelings will be generalized to include one another's values and opinions. In other words, a kind of emotional learning occurs.

An alternative strategy has a cognitive focus, where an effort is made to develop a common language with a good understanding of each other's values and opinions. In this process, participants will realize that they have many values in common. And they will recognize that most people have complex sets of values comprising many dimensions. This allows for a better dialogue between different groups, and incorrect and inaccurate myths about what characterizes "the others" are not so easily developed.

As we can see, it is possible to exercise value-based leadership in situations coloured by value conflicts. Although it is more challenging for both the formal leaders and the employees, it is important to recognize that this is part of the daily life in many professional organizations. Both the degree of the value base and the need for value development will then gain greater emphasis. This may ultimately have a positive impact on leadership processes.

7.6 Summary

The values which one develops when growing up are influenced by both socialization and education. These influences happen both in formal and informal settings. Values are subject to change over time and can be acquired through learning. Learning theory can be useful in understanding how this takes place. Cognitive theory stresses learning acquired through active reflection based upon experience. This means that values need to be inserted into the language of the individual. How the values are organized and clustered is important. Theories in use thus represent the knowledge which governs behaviour, whilst espoused theories are the knowledge made explicit. Furthermore, single and double-loop learning can help to understand how values are acquired and reinforced or challenged. Values do not operate in an emotional vacuum and factors such as conditioning will operate to both inculcate values and to extend them beyond their initial remit.

Values have been shown to have an important role in motivation. Motivation is an expression also of needs, and this chapter has explored various needs theories and their links to aspects of the professions. In particular, needs for self development, learning, and status can motivate professionals. The likelihood that a particular course of action will fulfil a particular need has also been discussed.

The role of emotions as a key element in values has also been explored. People evolve emotionally as they develop, and emotions can vary in strength and direction. Emotions can lead to associations with values and conditioning can take place from this association.

The chapter also provided a model of reflection involving a set of phases. Reflection is important in establishing and embedding ethical concepts. The possibility of change in values in organizations is also discussed using Schein's model of cultural change and transformation.

Finally, the challenge of dealing with conflicting values is addressed with an exploration of the effect of subcultures and different logics. The reality of most organizational situations is that conflicts in values will be found. A key task for the value-based leader is to understand these and resolve them.

Exercises for further development and understanding

- Think back to your childhood and upbringing. What values did you gain at an early age and how were these embedded in you? What experiences do you recall which strongly influenced your value set?
- How have any of your values developed over the years? If so, what were the influences which were associated with that change? Which ones were linked to educational experiences?
- Think back to a situation which challenged one of your values. Perhaps an experience in a work or social setting. How did you react to this? What were the emotions which were aroused and how did you deal with the situation? Did it lead to a change in your values?

Recommended further reading

Aadland, E. (2011). "The Ethical Reflection Process," in Aaland, E. & Matulayová, T. (eds) *Ethical Reflection in the Helping Professions*. Prešov: University of Prešov.

Alderfer, C.P. (1972). *Existence, Relatedness, and Growth*. New York: Free Press.

Argyris, C. & D. Scön (1978). *Organizational Learning: A Theory of Action Perspective*. Reading, MA: Addison Wesley.

Bandura, A. (1986). *Social Foundation of Thought and Action*. Englewood Cliffs, NJ: Prentice Hall.

Schein, E. (2010). *Organizational Culture and Leadership* (4. utg.). San Francisco, CA: Jossey Bass.

Part 3
Value-based leadership in practice

In Part 2, we developed a definition of value-based leadership, indicating that this form of leadership can be exercised at the individual, group, and organizational levels. In the last part of the book, the purpose is to show how this type of leadership can be used in practice. First, we shall introduce the concept of self-leadership, which is a crucial form of leadership in all professional work. Second, we look at team leadership, which is a common form of leadership in public professions. Finally, we evaluate transformational leadership. This leadership form has a clear value base, and thus appears as a value-based supplement to other, more traditional forms of leadership at the organizational level.

Self-leadership

8

Key learning points

At the end of this chapter the reader should be able to:

- appreciate how self-leadership takes place and understand the theoretical underpinning
- understand the organizational conditions for self-leadership to take place
- appreciate the strategies for self leadership
- be able to develop and practice self leadership.

In principle, self-leadership is performed by anyone who has independent room for action. In other words, they have a certain degree of latitude to make their own choices. Normally, formal leaders have the greatest room for action. They have been delegated the authority to make their own decisions and are responsible for the results that are generated. However, most workers have a certain amount of freedom in their job. This is especially true in the Nordic countries. As identified in an international survey, Nordic countries score highly on the dimension of participatory leadership – in other words, employees are actively pulled into the leadership process (Dorfman et al., 2004). In this context, professional employees are in a unique position. They must have the freedom to exercise professional judgement as a way to effectively execute their functions within the organization.

8.1 Self-leadership in a value-based perspective

The concept of self-leadership can be traced back to a 1986 article penned by Charles Manz (Manz, 1986). His intention was to develop a theory in which self-control was the central control mechanism. This was based on the recognition that within every organization, each employee has a strong influence on his or her own behaviour. No matter how many rules and control system are implemented, the individual employee will constantly be facing challenges and issues that need to be solved. Hence, it becomes important to study the processes underlying the decisions employees need to make.

Although the theories of self-leadership have received strong support (Neck & Houghton, 2006), they are also criticized. Much of the criticism is related to the theories not being differentiated enough from general theories of motivation and self-regulation. Critics argue that they do not offer any significantly new features (see ibid. for a review). In addition, the theories can be criticized for not having any explicit leadership perspective. It is taken for granted that leadership must be exercised in any situation where there is a problem that needs to be solved.

We believe that a more explicit leadership model will fruitfully complement the theories of self-leadership. In order to provide self-leadership with a more explicit grounding in values, we suggest the following definition:

> Value-based self-leadership is a goal-setting, problem-solving, language-creating, and value-developing interaction which is anchored in the organization's values and high ethical standards, and exercised at the individual level.

In other words, the general leadership process – with its focus on goal-setting, problem-solving, and creating language – also takes place in self-leadership. Note that the concept of interaction is still included in the definition, signifying that self-leadership is not necessarily practised in solitude. While many decisions must be made by each individual employee, there may be broad co-operation with colleagues. The same applies to language development. Language is not only necessary if we are to communicate with each other; it is also important when we need to reflect on how to handle a challenge in our work. Finally, the definition points out that self-leadership must be strongly anchored in the organization's values and high ethical standards.

Three important conditions for self-leadership are self-influence, self-control, and intrinsic work motivation (Manz, 1986). An employee who has *self-influence* has some independent freedom for action. Naturally, this room for action has its limits. A doctor, for example, has the authority to decide what treatment to give to a patient. However, the timing of the treatment must be adjusted to overarching rules – for example, a patient who has been diagnosed with cancer may be able to claim treatment within two weeks. Which decisions are assigned to specific positions may also vary over time. And the practices that have been developed may differ from the formal rules. However, a form of self-influence is necessary for the performance of self-leadership.

Self-control means that each individual employee should exercise discretion over his or her own decisions. For example, it is the teacher rather than the principal who must control the knowledge development of each individual student, the development of social relations in the classroom, or the development of students' sense of achievement. Self-control is thus a necessary condition for learning. Self-leadership is not just about deciding how to utilize the freedom for action; it is also about constantly making better decisions. When compared to a newly qualified teacher, an experienced teacher is normally better able to develop good relations between students. Self-control, however, does not mean the lack of external influence. Workers with a high level of self-control will also in some areas be controlled by formal leaders or superior authorities. For example, at a school, national tests are performed to check the level of knowledge among students, and student surveys are conducted to verify the quality of social relations in the class.

Intrinsic work motivation is created through the content of the job and not through external rewards. It is therefore related to the need for recognition, growth, and personal development (Alderfer, 1972). Here, both self-influence and self-control are important dimensions. An inner force or energy is created, which is a central element of professional work. If we apply a value-based element, this energy will be directed toward value-based objectives and value-based techniques for problem-solving. Emerging from this, the most important dimensions of self-leadership are compiled and presented in Figure 8.1.

On the basis of Figure 8.1, we can argue that in order to create good self-leadership and maintain an active self-leadership process, the value-based leadership process at the individual level must focus on developing a high degree of self-influence, self-control, and intrinsic work motivation.

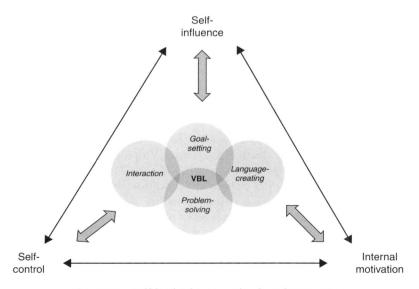

Figure 8.1   Self-leadership in a value-based perspective

8.2   Organizational requirements for self-leadership

So far we have made the assumption that self-leadership is suitable in professional organizations – whether it be healthcare, education, child protection, law enforcement, or other professional areas. But important questions are: Why is it suitable? What organizational factors are required for self-leadership to be an appropriate form of leadership?

Based on previous research, a model including three situational factors assumed to be important organizational requirements for self-leadership is developed (Houghton & Yoho, 2005). These factors are:

1. High follower readiness/maturity
2. Unstructured task environment
3. Low situational urgency.

The level of maturity among the employees is a complex factor that taps into their task-specific ability and willingness to perform a task. These constitute two important conditions for delegating tasks (Hersey & Blanchard, 1977). *Task specific ability* is related to an employee's level of expertise. This includes both knowledge and skills. While knowledge captures the cognitive component, skills represent the ability to perform the task in practice. *Willingness* is a bit more vague. It describes the employee's motivation, commitment, and ability to cope; that is, how much energy is put into performing the task. In other words, the model indicates that a high level of maturity is a prerequisite for self-leadership. Mature employees set ambitious goals, put in a lot of energy, and have solid academic qualifications for the job. They can as a consequence be given large autonomy in their work.

We must assume that professional employees to a large extent can be characterized by a high degree of maturity. Through specialized training and practical experience, they will score high on the ability to perform their duties. It does not mean that competence can be taken for granted. Anyone can become proficient – in terms of both knowledge and skill. However, professionals should have a sufficient basis for the knowledge they have, especially knowledge-based workers.

The willingness of employees is solidly tied to their values. If the organization's aims and means are clearly value-based, employees are both emotionally and motivationally prepared to do a good job. The motivation provides direction and emotion provides energy. On condition that the profession's core values are the basis for the organization's activities, we can assume that professional employees appear willing. The level of maturity should thus be high.

The structure of the task environment is more directly related to the character of the tasks. An unstructured task environment means that employees must decide for themselves how the job should be performed in practice. This also means that there is a high amount of uncertainty and a large space for action, and the tasks are most likely creative, analytical, or intellectual in character. The converse consists of highly structured tasks, where a series of rules are set up for how to perform them. The structure of the task environment can never be calculated exactly, although it does give an indication of how much freedom is associated with a task. Therefore, the term is largely equal to what we previously referred to as room for action. While room for action is related to a person, degree of freedom is more related to a task. The model indicates that a sufficient degree of freedom in executing a task is an important prerequisite for the suitability of self-leadership.

As previously mentioned, professional occupations are characterized by a great deal of autonomy. Many of the tasks are highly complex, and discretion is exercised when performing the work. Generally, this means a high degree of freedom when executing tasks. At the same time, a variety of rules and procedures must also be followed as a way to ensure equal treatment. For example, both doctors and nurses are constrained by a number of rules at the hospital. Still, while Broadbent & Laughlin (2002) demonstrate that professional organizations in the public sector have been faced with a rise in the use of bureaucratic rules, public-sector professionals still have a large amount of freedom in task performance, which points to the active use of self-leadership.

The last factor identified by Houghton and Yoho (2005) is related to time pressure. The model assumes the possibility of a more direct form of leadership being needed, especially in crisis situations. A co-ordinated effort is required, and it is argued that instead of self-leadership, other forms of leadership are more equipped to deal with crisis episodes. However, this part of the model can be questioned. Critical situations can occur – for example at a hospital – where self-leadership is still the best form of leadership. In this case, the problem must be solved by those who are closest to the patient and who have the highest professional competence. There are also examples where self-organizing works quickly and effectively in major crisis situations that lack a centralized leadership. We will not be discussing this here, although we do assume that self-leadership works well in situations with low situational urgency.

There is also a host of research on the effects of self-leadership (Houghton & Yoho, 2005; Neck & Houghton, 2006). The primary effects include increasing:

1. Commitment and independence
2. Self-efficacy
3. Trust and team potency
4. Job satisfaction
5. Creativity and innovation
6. Psychological empowerment.

High commitment means that the employee has a strong emotional and identity-related connection with their workplace. It is well documented that this has a positive effect on job satisfaction, job involvement, and performance levels (see Riketta, 2005 for a review). In addition, there are strong indications that self-leadership creates high levels of self-efficacy; that is, the employees gain

Figure 8.2   Important requirements for self-leadership

increased confidence in their ability to deal with the challenges of the job. There is also evidence that self-leadership creates greater trust and team potency, which is critical for facilitating team effectiveness. Finally, self-leadership has a positive effect on job satisfaction and creates independent, creative, and empowered employees.

The model is not empirically tested, but is based on extensive research over the course of many years. This indicates that self-leadership may be well suited for public-sector, knowledge-based organizations which are largely influenced by professional workers. The model is shown in Figure 8.2.

Example 14

Traffic enforcement by camera

Many countries have moved on from enforcement of speeding by camera to enforcement of parking and other traffic issues by camera. The use of automation for this removes much of the discretion which operated when these activities were undertaken by staff. On the one hand, it means that regulations are exercised according to set rules without favour or partiality. However, it also means that the exercise of discretion is not so possible. There is no opportunity for the motorist to explain to an official at the time of the infraction and to see the exercise of discretion in whether a penalty is appropriate. Equally, the impersonality of the process means that the official is unable to engage in any discourse with the motorist which may lead to a more positive perception of the rationale for a penalty being applied.

8.3   Strategies for self-leadership

Given the fact that self-leadership is based on self-influence, self-direction, and self-motivation, a set of more specific strategies is developed in order to expand this leadership model (Manz & Neck, 2004). These strategies are divided into three main groups:

1.   Behaviour-focused strategies
2.   Natural reward strategies
3.   Constructive thought pattern strategies.

Behaviour-focused strategies are aimed at increasing awareness of how one's own behaviour affects the degree of goal achievement. Among other things, self-observation, self-goal setting, self-reward, and self-punishment can be used as specific strategies. Through self-observation, it is possible to reflect more systematically on one's own behaviour. A teacher can, for example, write down how he tackles different challenges in the classroom, including critical challenges or situations which require actions that are perceived as unpleasant. When used retrospectively, the teacher can reflect on whether or not the behaviour was appropriate in terms of realizing important objectives, thus providing a crucial venue for changing behaviour. This activity can be combined with self-goal setting – both for one's own performance and for one's own behaviour. There is good research evidence that the formulation of objectives can influence the level of performance (Locke & Latham, 1990). For these to influence behaviour, they need to be well anchored in one's own values; if they are, they will create both energy and motivation.

Self-reward can have the same effect, especially when it comes to the realization of one's own goals. It creates focus and becomes a symbol of a good performance. The reward can be as simple as a teacher saying to herself, "You handled this student very well." Or it can be a more tangible reward like inviting a good colleague out for lunch. The purpose of using self-punishment is to raise awareness of why something went wrong. It may be an important strategy in some situations, although it may create an unfortunate negative attention and should not be used too often (Manz & Sims, 2001). There is good research evidence showing that these techniques affect job performance levels. When implementing these strategies into a value-based context, it should be considered whether our own behaviour is consistent with the central norms and values of the organization.

The purpose of *natural reward strategies* is to create a situation in which employees experience intrinsic motivation when performing their tasks. A distinction can be made between two main categories. In the first category, the aim is to add multiple motivational factors into the job. The question is thus how to make a job that might be somewhat boring more exciting. Is it possible to add some learning opportunities, some pleasant social meetings, raise the bar or create more academic challenges?

In the second category, the purpose is to influence one's own perceptions in order to shift the focus from negative to positive aspects of the job. Perception is how we experience and interpret our emotions. Although this can be a difficult strategy, it can open up a realization that the job has multiple dimensions. Negative aspects can attract so much attention that the positive aspects "disappear." Thus, positive aspects must gain focus while negative aspects are pushed back. These strategies are believed to influence the feeling of competence and self-determination – two important mechanisms for creating internal motivation. Trivial and unrewarding tasks can become meaningful by being placed into a larger value-based context.

The purpose of *constructive thought pattern strategies* is to develop thought patterns that elicit positive effects on performance levels. Among other things, this includes identification of dysfunctional beliefs about our own performance.

Negative thoughts pertaining to future challenges should, according to these strategies, be replaced with more positive thinking patterns. The focus is set on what is called positive self-talk – that is, the silent discussions people have with themselves when conducting various tasks.

For example, a child-welfare consultant may have developed a low self-esteem that manifests when confronting resourceful parents, and unpleasant thoughts begin each time the consultant meets them. In such settings, the expectations are set high, and the consultant is afraid of not doing an adequate job. But the real challenge is to break this pattern of thought. First, it must be acknowledged that these obsessive thoughts are dysfunctional; they create a poor starting point and may even contribute to making the meetings unsuccessful. Then, these negative thoughts need to be replaced with positive thoughts about the meeting. The consultant must convince herself about her ability to handle the meetings. To enhance this process, she should talk with talented colleagues or be even more prepared before meeting the parents.

This can be combined with the development of positive affirmations of future performance. To be sure, research has shown that such affirmations to a large degree affect subsequent performance (Driskell et al., 1994). The child-care consultant may for instance try to form pictures of how the family in question can best be assisted, and what positive progress the child may have. The goal here, like the one described in the paragraph above, is to improve performance by stopping negative thought patterns and by reinforcing positive ones.

8.4   Developing self-leadership

Within the field of leadership research, self-leadership is primarily tied to empowering leadership. This is defined as a process aimed at helping others to lead themselves (Manz & Sims, 1991, 2001).

First of all, efforts must be made to render self-leadership suitable. This especially applies to the development of employee maturity and the degree of freedom in task execution. When it comes to maturity, a satisfactory *competence* among employees must be developed early on. Although basic skills are in place, there is always a need for further training. New tasks, new user groups, new challenges, and new technologies require continuous competence development. Self-leadership requires employees to have the necessary knowledge, skills, and the ability to master new challenges.

Second, employees must be *willing* to maintain active self-leadership. Here, it must be emphasized that self-leadership is different to merely maintaining task independence. Empowerment is implicit in most professional jobs. But self-leadership goes beyond this by requiring an awareness of which objectives must be realized and which methods are most suitable for them. Willingness means that employees want to exercise self-leadership; they must therefore have an inner drive directed towards leadership. As previously mentioned, this may be realized by tightly integrating the profession's values with the organization's objectives and means. Such integration may necessitate the challenge of making adjustments to both the value base and the objectives/measures. It is, however, hard to find a shortcut in that direction.

Finally, the tasks must be of such a nature that self-leadership can be exercised. This means that the job must have a large degree of freedom. Each employee must have a scope for action that is broad enough to be relevant for self-leadership. At the same time, this breadth can be a dilemma for the organization's formal leaders. Strong demands for standardization of work processes and documentation can reduce the employee's room for action (Broadbent & Laughlin, 2007; Busch & Dehlin, 2012). Therefore, to the extent possible, formal leaders must try to influence the external requirements that impinge upon leadership, so that appropriate self-leadership is not blocked.

Developing active self-leadership among employees can be a long process, and it is not always sufficient to facilitate the conditions just by cultivating maturity and providing broad degrees of freedom. Some additional recommendations are (Manz & Sims, 1991):

1. Become a self-leader.
2. Model self-leadership.
3. Encourage self-set goals.
4. Create positive thought patterns.

The first recommendation indicates that in order to develop sufficient self-leadership, the formal leader needs to know what it is all about. The formal leader must therefore become a self-leader, which includes both knowledge of it and skills in it. In practice, this means that the leader must try to use all three strategies for self-leadership that were discussed in the previous section. If the leader does not have the necessary knowledge, it is difficult to convey to others how self-leadership can be exercised.

The second recommendation is largely based on the theory of model learning (Bandura, 1986). It points out that we learn just as much from observing others as we do from our own experiences. This applies, first of all, to seeing what others are doing, and then to listening to what others say. In other words, we copy both behaviour and thought patterns. An important prerequisite for this learning to occur is for the models to have a sufficiently high status. Formal leaders with high social standing among their employees may act as good role models.

A formal leader who wants to develop self-leadership must therefore demonstrate what this means in practice – either through their own behaviour or by explaining how it is done. Since strategies for self-leadership are primarily related to self-reflection, the latter can be the most appropriate. Hence, the leader must communicate to her employees the ways in which she carries out self-leadership in practice. This must be as specific as possible in order to give the employees a great opportunity for model learning. It is here essential that the leader demonstrates the personal rewards that self-leadership can create. This will greatly enhance the learning. When we observe models getting rewarded, we unconsciously assume (learn) that we get the same rewards by copying the model.

The third and fourth recommendations further support this process. The leader can, first of all, encourage employees to develop their own goals, either directly or by implementing processes where employees work jointly with goal development. This can also be integrated with discussions of objectives, where the focus is set on the relationship between the overall objectives and the objectives each individual has to work on. Secondly, the leader can actively attempt to create positive thought patterns. Negative thoughts are often developed in social contexts. They are created in a joint venture, and can easily be enhanced by new employees joining with their support. The leader can attempt to show that in practice, negative thought patterns are dysfunctional. They may inhibit motivation, weaken work enthusiasm, and contribute to poorer results. By contrast, positive thought patterns can be introduced as an alternative. If the formal leader is conscious of keeping a positive focus, over time this can weaken negative thought patterns and thereby improve the opportunities for an active self-leadership.

8.5   Summary

Leadership is not always leadership of people or resources. It can also be self-leadership. Self-leadership can be traced back to a concept of self-control as the key mechanism. For this to happen it is necessary to have some room for action. This may be substantial, such as deciding whether even to undertake an assignment, or it may be more restricted, such as the decision about how to address an individual when you meet them. It is argued that such self-leadership is particularly relevant for both professional settings and public-sector organizations where values are strongly held and where the individual member of staff is regarded as having significant discretion. There are factors in both the individual and the organization which can promote or impede self-leadership. It is feasible to adopt strategies to maximize self-leadership and to practise it effectively. It is important to be aware of the factor which might encourage (or impede) self-leadership. There are various strategies which can assist self-leadership and these can be seen as focusing on behaviour, natural reward, or constructive thought patterns. Using these strategies can empower and encourage self-leadership. However, it is important to recognize that the process can be a long one and this chapter offers recommendations to enable it to happen.

Exercises for further development and understanding

- Consider how much independent room for action you have in your work situation. How would you be aware of this and how might you measure it?
- List three tasks which you regularly undertake as part of your work. How much freedom do you have in doing them? Think about the key words "when, how, where and who" to help you decide.

- How would you change things in your organization in order to enable more "self-leadership?" What might be the advantages and the disadvantages of doing so?

Recommended further reading

Houghton, J.D. & Yoho, S.K. (2005). "Toward a Contingency Model of Leadership and Psychological Empowerment: When Should Self-Leadership Be Encouraged"? *Journal of Leadership & Organizational Studies*, 11, 65–83.

Manz, C.C. & Neck, C.P. (2004). *Mastering Self-Leadership: Empowering Yourself for Personal Excellence* (Third edition). Upper Saddle River, NJ: Prentice Hall.

Neck, C.P. & Houghton, J.D. (2006). "Two Decades of Self-Leadership Theory and Research. Past Developments, Present Trends, and Futures Possibilities," *Journal of Managerial Psychology*, 21, 270–295.

Team leadership

9

Key learning points

At the end of this chapter the reader should be able to:

- understand what a team is and what its characteristics should be
- know what is associated with high performance in teams
- locate team leadership in a value-based perspective
- appreciate how a good team is developed and be able to plan for how this is done.

Team organizing is often used in professional organizations. In a wide array of contexts it is understood as an appropriate form of pulling together people for task execution (Busch & Dehlin, 2012). While many professionals work independently, there is a growing need for collaboration, including collaboration with other organizations. Indeed, network solutions have become increasingly widespread in the public sector (Sørensen, 2007). Teams and project groups are established with members from several organizations, which can provide both flexibility and robust results (Sørensen, 2007). We will therefore take a closer look at value-based leadership in a team context.

9.1   What is a team?

Teams are flexible organizational forms that have received much attention in recent years, and a range of models have been developed, aiming at understanding the processes contributing to increased efficiency (Assmann, 2008; Bang, 2008;

Katzenbach & Smith, 1998; Sjøvold, 2010). Significant importance is attached to distinguishing between a workgroup and a team, where the greatest difference is that the former does not have a clear objective for which all participants strive (Katzenbach & Smith, 1998). Members are therefore less dependent on each other. They meet primarily to share information and discuss various challenges. They can support each other in order to make good decisions within their own jurisdiction; however, they do not have joint responsibility for the obtained results.

For example, all the mathematics teachers at a high school can form a group to co-ordinate exams and tests. They can also bring to the group various issues they face in their respective classes. But does this really constitute teamwork? The answer is "no" since they lack a clear commitment to realizing any common goals. This is primarily described as a workgroup rather than a team. If this group is asked to make an analysis of the educational principles used in teaching mathematics at school, with the purpose of making suggestions for change, the group would then look more like an actual team organization. At that point, the group of educators would have a common goal and produce concrete results that the school's principal would evaluate.

In practice, there is a gradual transition between a workgroup and a team. At one end, we have a traditional workgroup, where there are no common tasks. At the other end, we have what is called a high-performance team, where members are strongly committed in terms of the team's success and development (Katzenbach & Smith, 1998). Between these two extremes, we find many different group types with greater and lesser degrees of "team-ness."

Working in a team is significantly more demanding than working in a workgroup. The obligations are larger, and a far greater emphasis is placed on leadership. However, it is also more rewarding for the individual, and it provides better results for the organization. Despite these advantages, it is important to keep in mind that both workgroups and teams are necessary for an organization. The form selected depends on the task to be solved.

Overall, team organizing is best under the following conditions (Pearce, 2004):

- interdependency
- creativity
- complexity.

A high level of employee interdependence means that they influence each other's potential for creating results. An example can be a group of soldiers with the responsibility for carrying out a specific mission. They all depend on each other to achieve a good outcome. None of them can do a proper job without co-ordination with the other soldiers.

If there is an urgent need for creativity, then team organizing may be appropriate. The reason for this is that new and innovative solutions may come about when people with various backgrounds work together. They will challenge one another, and new approaches may surface. For example, a team charged with assessing the methods used within child-welfare organizations might consist of two child-welfare workers, two social workers, a psychologist, a psychiatrist, a lawyer, and a specialist in organizational behaviour. This diversity of backgrounds can enable creative dynamics that would hardly unfold if this task were assigned to a single officer within child welfare.

If the task has a high level of complexity, there is little chance that one person will have the necessary skills to find an adequate solution. Complex and intricate tasks often require knowledge from several disciplines, and a team can therefore be well suited for this. For example, the police are appointed to develop better methods for handling organized crime. Organized crime is built up from an integration of legal and illegal activities; for example, money laundering. The solutions are complex and diverse, and it is unlikely that one person alone can come up with an adequate solution for tackling this particular form of crime.

In these situations, a team will probably provide the best solution. What are the characteristics of a team? We will use the following definition:

A team is a small number of people with complementary skills who are highly committed to a common purpose, performance goals, and approach, for which they hold themselves mutually accountable. (Katzenbach & Smith, 1998, p. 45)

This is a complicated definition that includes:

- a small number of people
- complementary skills
- commitment to a common purpose and performance goals
- commitment to a common approach
- mutual accountability.

Let us now take a closer look at what these points entail.

A small number of people

The number of people in the team is important; it should not be too large. On the one hand, if a team has too many members, it becomes more difficult to develop a strong commitment among them. Likewise, the level of social control is weaker and team members can "sneak away" more easily. On the other hand, if a team is too small there may be limited expertise and energy within the group. As such, a team size of five to six people is often recommended (Hackman, 2002; Katzenbach & Smith, 1998), although a team of ten to fifteen may also work well, depending on the nature of the task. There is a trade-off between ensuring good processes and ensuring adequate expertise in the team.

Complementary skills

Within a team, an adequate mixture of skills must be present in order for the task to be sufficiently concluded. This is especially important when tasks are complex or require a high degree of creativity. We can distinguish between *professional, leadership, and relational* skills (Katzenbach & Smith, 1998). All these skills should be present within a team. Professional skills are tied to the specific task that is being solved. Leadership skills are necessary for developing a satisfactory team leadership process. Therefore, members must be able to work systematically in both goal-setting and problem-solving. And if necessary, they must develop a common language that is suitable for sound interaction between the members.

Finally, there is a need for relational skills. It is necessary to cultivate a climate where members can deal with disagreements, conflicts, and criticism, while still caring for and supporting one another. In other words, the team needs to function as a strong social group. Because the team must focus on both the task at hand and the relations between members, it is important that someone in the team has skills and insight into developing socio-emotional relations.

Commitment to a common purpose and performance goals

Team development requires a common vision and a common goal. While the vision indicates the overall purpose of the teamwork, the goal delineates the specificities of the desired achievements. For the team to function optimally, both vision and goals need full support. Although others can impose visions and goals on the team, these impositions must be interpreted and developed by the team. A common understanding of the team's purpose and the results to be achieved must be created. It is an important and potentially time-consuming process, and there is no guarantee that all members of the team start off by agreeing on what constitutes the most important objectives. If the team cannot agree on common goals, it will be difficult to generate the necessary momentum for the team to function. This process can continue over the long run, as visions and objectives may be interpreted and re-interpreted throughout the team's existence. Continuity in vision and objectives along with proper motivations constitute an important basis for how the team evaluates itself.

Commitment to a common approach

The team's members must figure out the best way to work together in order to realize their objectives. They also need to agree on which professional approach to take. This can be quite specific and include requirements for attendance, preparation, effort, and contributions; divisions of responsibility; and demands for mutual respect. Altogether, these agreements will serve as the norms that regulate the team's work. Provisions must be made for discussing norm violations. In addition, there should be some form of common professional approach to the task. Various approaches must naturally be considered, which in itself can be a lengthy process. In the end, however, the team should agree on and commit to one key strategy – or a few strategies.

Mutual accountability

The last point in the definition indicates that the team members are mutually accountable for common visions, goals, and approaches – perhaps best captured by the phrase "all for one and one for all." Everyone is responsible for the results which are obtained. Members must commit to each other and be confident that everyone contributes the required effort. This must be expressed both internally in the team and in relation to external stakeholders. Creating mutual accountability necessitates a commitment to shared visions, goals, and approaches. If this fails, it becomes far more difficult to develop a sense of mutual responsibility. In other words, it is not simply the individual who is responsible for his or her performance within the team. Rather, everyone must jointly take responsibility for the team's performance.

The definition specifies five criteria that can be used to assess whether a group should be considered a team. This also gives meaning for talking about the extent of "teamness," or the degree to which a group meets these five criteria. In other words, in order to be a genuine team, a group should score reasonably well on all these points. The definition also indicates that a group can continuously strive towards becoming a genuine team. In this case, the definition highlights a number of important dimensions that need to be worked on along the way.

In addition to genuine teams that largely satisfy this definition, the term "high-performance teams" is also used. This describes teams that generate extremely good results (Katzenbach & Smith, 1998; Søholm & Juhl, 2005). In addition to satisfying all the specified criteria in the definition, these teams are characterized by *a deep commitment to each other's personal growth and success.* The obligation is not just to the team but to helping each other to achieve personal and professional goals, which, according to some, will transform the genuine team into a new form that produces high-performance results. This mutual assistance also enhances the dimensions in the specified definition. The members will feel a stronger commitment to the team, and more challenging goals will be formulated.

9.2   Team leadership in a value-based perspective

The definition of a team shows that team members need to engage strongly in both goal-setting (common vision and goals) and problem-solving (common approach). This entails developing a shared responsibility for leadership processes. We might call it shared leadership between all members (Pearce, 2004). The definition also indicates that values are of great importance. To provide robust commitment and accountability, both emotional and motivational dimensions are important, thus anchoring the leadership process to the value base.

Although the theories of team leadership are clearly linked to a leadership perspective, they are only built to a small degree on an explicit leadership model. To complement this, we choose to apply our general definition:

> Team leadership is a goal-setting, problem-solving, language-creating, and value-developing interaction, which is anchored in the organization's values and high ethical standards at the group level.

This means that goal-setting, problem-solving, and language-creating are also central elements in the leadership processes within a team. The definition is, as we can see, only linked to the group level. This implies that these leadership processes take place within a tight environment. Moreover, the value element is marked by referring to the organization's values and ethical standards. In other words, when it comes to values, the team must be adequately integrated into the organization it is a part of, thereby giving birth to a specific team culture. The team must therefore develop a set of values that governs members' behaviours – both in terms of terminal values and instrumental values. To do so, key objectives and norms must have moorings that include motivational and emotional components.

A major challenge follows when a team consists of members from several independent organizations, at which point the team must also cultivate a commitment to common values – not just a common vision, goal, and approach. Values must be made explicit, and the leadership process related to language creation is of crucial importance. The most significant challenge arises when public agencies are to co-operate with non-governmental or private organizations. In these cases, their value bases can be very different – not necessarily in all dimensions, but there arguably some basic public-sector values that are not prevalent in the other two sectors.

Theories of team leadership contain a multitude of elements that have a value basis. We will take a closer look at those theories that attempt to bridge the divide between self-leadership and team leadership. This bridge is interesting since self-leadership is important for all team members. Team members do not just work together but must often conduct a large part of the job alone. Stated differently, satisfactory self-leadership is important for teamwork not only because it creates better results; self-leadership is also connected to many other dimensions (Houghton & Yoho, 2005; Neck & Houghton, 2006), including the strength of organizational commitment and the level of trust and self-efficacy. Having people with competent self-leadership skills meet in a team setting will transfer these skills over to the team level, thus helping to strengthen team commitment, team trust, and team efficacy (Bligh et al., 2006). In short, self-leadership is beneficial because it will increase:

- individual trust, which will increase team trust
- self-efficacy, which will increase team efficacy
- organizational commitment, which will increase team commitment.

The concepts of team trust, team efficacy, and team commitment are key elements in a well-functioning team. All three concepts are robustly anchored in values. Team trust indicates that members should develop a high level of relational security, which includes openness to addressing relationship issues and personal affairs, and a sense of confidence in not being humiliated (Edmondson, 1999). We distinguish between emotionally based trust and cognitively based trust (McAllister, 1995). Emotionally based trust is developed through social relations and forms the basis for sharing personal information. Cognitively based trust is created as team members see that the others act professionally and can be relied upon when the job needs to be done. Both forms of team trust must be present because the first is the basis for developing the socio-emotional climate within the team, and the other is the basis for a well-functioning, task-solving process. A high degree of self-leadership is believed to have a positive effect on cognitively based trust.

Previously we have shown that self-efficacy is related to social learning theory. It is created by a person who repeatedly masters specific challenges, which is why self-leadership leads to improved abilities at mastering other things. It is expected that these abilities will be transferred to the team level: when individuals meet to solve challenges which are relevant to their strong sense of efficacy, a powerful belief coalesces around the team's collective ability to deal with the challenge. People with high levels of self-efficacy will choose challenging activities; they will expend lots of energy in addressing the tasks, and they will endure a greater number of complications and obstacles in the process without giving up. Transferring this to the team level, we see that the level of team efficacy will have a major impact on team performance.

A strong feeling of organizational commitment is characterized by a strong acceptance of organizational goals and values, a strong willingness to work on behalf of the organization, and a strong desire to maintain membership within the organization (Mowday et al., 1979). Transferring this to team thinking, we see that team commitment is a very important dimension in teamwork. It means that every member has a strong commitment to the team's values, visions, and goals. We can say that it creates a strong team spirit that captures members' emotional connections with each other (Forsyth, 2006; Mullen & Copper, 1994). Membership is important, and the members are proud to be part of the team. It can be argued that there are close links between organizational commitment and team commitment. When the team is part of the organization, it is seen as highly valuable by individuals with strong organizational commitment. Thus, the basis for strong team commitment is also created.

Given the fact that team trust, team efficacy, and team commitment are very important dimensions in a functioning team, and they are clearly tied to the team's value base, we will implement these dimensions into an extended model of team leadership, which is illustrated in Figure 9.1.

Thus, it can be argued that self-leadership and team leadership are highly interrelated. Those with effective self-leadership will provide a solid basis for the development of effective teams. Since professionals usually work in a way that promotes self-leadership, team leadership should be well suited to professional organizations. Moreover, value-based self-leadership provides a sound foundation for developing team leadership that has a clear value base and ethical foundation.

Example 15

Bay of Pigs

In 1961, President Kennedy made what he later regarded as one of the biggest mistakes of his presidency when he sanctioned an abortive invasion of Cuba by a group of Cuban exiles. The attempt has been described as one of the few examples of "perfect failure" yet the American politicians and their advisors who agreed to it could not be described as foolish men. So how did it happen? A psychologist, Irving Janus, coined the term "groupthink" to explain it. In the interests of conformity and team cohesion, advisors, even though some were unsure of the wisdom of the invasion, agreed with the decision to invade.

One advisor who was more adamantly opposed to the invasion was not included in a vote of advisors sought by Kennedy. One aspect which may have been relevant was that the invasion was planned during the term of Kennedy's predecessor, and the group of advisors, having committed to the course of action, may have been reluctant to accept evidence which clearly indicated that it was likely to fail. Rather, they were prone to favour information (provided by the CIA, which was positive about the invasion). Kennedy drew lessons from the experience. When, some years after, he confronted the Cuban Missile Crisis (when Russia provided missiles to Cuba capable of reaching the US mainland), Kennedy was careful to ensure that he received and encouraged a diversity of advice and held back from the more extreme courses of action advocated by some advisors.

Group-think could be seen in the trust put in evidence of "weapons of mass destruction" in Iraq, which led to an invasion which some regard as ill-advised and inappropriate. The evidence was subsequently viewed as having dubious provenance.

9.3   How to develop a good team?

We will end this chapter by looking more closely at how to develop a well-functioning team. It is impossible to come up with a recipe that will work in every situation, because social organizations are always to some extent unpredictable. These

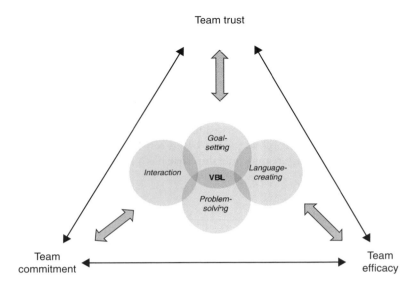

Team trust

Team commitment

Team efficacy

Goal-setting

Interaction   VBL   Language-creating

Problem-solving

Figure 9.1   Team leadership in a value-based perspective

recommendations must therefore be considered as inputs to a development process (Katzenbach & Smith, 1998).

Start the work immediately

It is vital to set out a clear direction and, to some extent at least, highlight the urgency of the work. This will immediately place the participants in a good frame of mind for carrying out the work. The focus is prepared, and the team will get to work quickly. It is more important to start the process as quickly as possible, as opposed to spending a lot of time getting to know each other. While trust and transparency are important, these are better created through hands-on teamwork rather than using a lot of time in the beginning to develop social relations.

Select members based on skills and not personality

It is essential to have the necessary expertise in place in order for the team to function well. Expertise should weigh the most if selecting the participating members is an option. In addition, strong emphasis should be placed on the opportunities for members to further develop their own professional, leadership, and relational competencies. Indeed, when seen in the long-term perspective of the organization's skill portfolio, competence development may be equally important as the current competencies. Besides, opportunities for improving competencies will help motivate members.

The first phase of teamwork is particularly important

The start-up and the first team meetings require special attention. Notions and roles that have a lasting influence on teamwork are created during this time. This applies particularly to the vision and long-term goals. Key questions are:

- What shall the team achieve?
- What direction should it take?
- What is the guiding value basis?

This early stage creates future notions and provides for a primary focus for the work. For similar reasons, the initial communications and impression made by a team leader are especially important. The leader's basic authority is powerful, and during the first phase, the team members are very aware of the signals given out.

Set up clear rules of action

Quickly set the focus on how the team will work together. What rules will be applied? What values should the work be based on? What behaviours are desired? During the first phase, all members look for signals about these issues, and they try to express their own opinions about them. Eventually, a set of policy rules, which will affect the teamwork will crystallize. It is important that these rules are adequate and provide a good framework for addressing the given tasks. When these rules are set, they can be difficult to change. Therefore, strong attention is required from both the team leader and the other members in this first phase.

Quickly establish some short-term performance goals

Teams often get a boost of energy from performance-oriented goals. And short-term goals provide an easy way to jump-start the work. These goals must also be challenging – the team must strive to achieve results. The goals may even be challenging enough for the team to debate whether or not they are realistic. Higher objectives will generate energy and are motivating in themselves. They stimulate collaboration and create good learning processes. It is not always necessary for these short-term goals to be realized – their main function may be to create energy and get the processes started.

The team should be challenged regularly with new information

In a team, it is easy to get caught up in the idea of being on the right track – the team has found *The Solution*. This can reduce the team's energy level, as the members relax and focus more on the group's social life. This can be unfortunate, especially if the group is not on the right path. Bringing new information to the table – information which challenges their way of thinking – can help sustain the energy level. The team must defend their solutions, find new approaches, or redefine their tasks. New information sets in motion a new learning process, and continuous learning is perhaps the most important element of the team process.

Spend a lot of time together

It is crucial, especially at the beginning, for the team to spend time together. This can be both formally and informally in social settings. It is necessary to develop a well-functioning team culture, trusting relationships, feelings of team belongingness, and strong collective efficacy, all of which necessitate time together. Although the workday is busy, teamwork should be prioritized, especially since a high-performance team requires good personal relationships.

Emphasize positive feedback and recognition

Teamwork provides a variety of internal rewards; for example, learning opportunities, personal growth, involvement, and social relations. This also facilitates strong motivation. However, external rewards should also be utilized, such as recognition and praise for good performance. Everyone needs to know that they are valued and that they do a good job.

Although these suggestions highlight important aspects of the process around team development, there is no standard recipe for success. In general, we can say that it is important to stay focused on the elements embedded in the team definition and the value-based leadership process. With these elements as a foundation, our recommendations can stimulate further learning.

9.4   Summary

The concept of the team is central to most organizations. A team is distinct from a workgroup insofar as the former possesses a clear commitment to realizing common goals, and team organizing is best under conditions of interdependency, creativity, and complexity (Pearce, 2004).

Teams possess particular characteristics, namely *a small number of people with complementary skills who are highly committed to a common purpose, performance goals, and approach, for which they hold themselves mutually accountable* (Katzenbach & Smith 1998, p. 45). This chapter examined each aspect of this definition in some detail, and the components of this definition can be used to assess the degree of "teamness."

Mutual commitment to shared visions, goals, and approaches is one significant factor behind team success. Two other factors are team trust and team efficacy. Finally, the bridges and links between self-leadership and team leadership are important for developing a well-functioning team. Hence, team trust, efficacy, and commitment can be seen as supportive of the extended model of team leadership which we have defined as goal-setting, problem-solving, language-creating, and value-developing interaction anchored in the organization's values and high ethical standards at the group level.

There are principles which, if followed, can assist in effectively setting up and running teams. The start-up phase is especially important with the establishment of clear rules and short-term performance goals. It is important for a team to be challenged and to spend a lot of time together. Feedback and recognition can foster internal rewards though external rewards should not be neglected. At the same time, the range and diversity of organizational situations mean that there is no assurance that one particular approach will guarantee success.

Exercises for further development and understanding

- When talking with a colleague who regards a workgroup and a team as the same, how would you explain the differences?
- If you were asked in your workplace to form a team to resolve a problem, how would you set about doing this? What steps would you take?
- Think about two situations you have experienced in a team, where one situation has been much more successful than the other. List the reasons why you think there was a difference between the two experiences. Assess whether the use of team leadership concepts might have improved the less successful team situation.

Recommended further reading

Bligh, M.C., Pearce, C.L. & Kohles, J.C. (2006). "The Importance of Self- and Shared Leadership in Team Based Knowledge Work. A Meso-Level Model of Leadership Dynamics," *Journal of Managerial Psychology*, 21, 4, 296–318.

Katzenbach, J.R. & Smith, D.K. (1998). *The Wisdoms of Teams*. London: McGraw Hill.

Pearce, C.L. (2004). "The Future of Leadership: Combining Vertical and Shared Leadership to Transform Knowledge Work," *Academy of Management Executive*, 18, 47–57.

Transformational leadership

10

Key learning points

At the end of this chapter the reader should:

- understand what distinguishes transformational leadership, transactional leadership, and laissez-faire leadership
- be aware of the components and characteristics of transformational leadership and in particular the importance of values and vision for it
- be able to discuss the importance of vision for transformational leadership.

Transformational leadership has a clear value base and is therefore largely associated with value-based leadership (MacTavish & Kolb, 2008). The main objective of transformational leadership is to motivate employees, who will be "transformed" into a higher level of morale and motivation and place organizational goals in front of their own interests. Research has shown that this form of leadership seems to occur more frequently in organic organizations (Bass, 1985; Quinn, 1988); that is to say, organizations where the impact of formal rules is minimal. In these organizations the division of responsibilities may vary over time, and areas of responsibility are not simply limited to those given by formal definitions. Rather, transformational leadership is conceptualized with a broad sense of responsibility, and thus accountability. Likewise, jobs are continuously redefined through collaboration (Burns & Stalker, 1961). Furthermore, it is also well documented that transformational leadership seems to work well in highly professional organizations (see review in Bass, 2008). Transformational leadership should therefore be very relevant for leading professional employees.

10.1   What distinguishes transformational leadership?

The concept of transformational leadership can largely be attributed to Burns (1978), who wrote a book about political leadership. In his definition, transformational leadership is described as a process whereby leaders and employees lift each other up to a higher level. As such, transformational leaders appeal to lofty ideals and moral values like freedom, justice, equality, peace, and humanism. They enable more powerful motives and lift employees from their "everyday selves" to their "better selves." Although this form of leadership can be performed at all levels of the organization, it is primarily focused on executives who sit in formal positions. Heavy emphasis is placed on the leader's values and how this is communicated throughout the organization. We can therefore consider transformational leadership as value-based leadership exercised at the organizational level.

Transformational leadership can also be linked to the leader's ability to express a value-based vision that creates a moral commitment among employees (House, 1996). An important assumption is that the leadership must be based on a stated ideological objective, which can challenge the status quo. Moreover, the leader's values must, to a certain degree, be in accordance with the internalized values of the organization, the organization must be in the midst of some sort of crisis, and a special effort is required from both leaders and employees.

A key point in this theory is that transformational leadership is radically different from what might be seen as its opposite; that is, transactional leadership (Bass, 2008). In addition, a third form of leadership is pulled into the theory – namely "laissez-faire-leadership" (Avolio & Bass, 1991). Out of these three forms of leadership, transformational leadership is considered to be most active, while "laissez-faire" leadership is considered to be the most passive.

Transformational leadership

Thus, transformational leadership emphasizes that the employees shall: (a) be aware of both terminal and instrumental values; (b) rise above their own self-interests for the benefit of overall objectives; and (c) focus on the higher-level needs for achievement and self-actualization (Burns, 1978). This form of leadership thus appears with many positive elements. Both leaders and employees should realize their potential while working for the overall goals and visions. Based on Burns's original theories, more complete theories of transformational leadership have been developed, which consist of four main components (Bass & Avolio, 1993):

1. *Idealized influence.* This assumes that the leader has strong charisma, which is valued by employees.
2. *Inspirational motivation.* The leaders motivate employees to strive for visions and overall goals.
3. *Intellectual stimulation.* The leaders challenge employees to take new paths and find innovative solutions.

4. *Individualized consideration*. The leaders show concern for the employees, encourage a good working environment, and support employees in their individual development.

Transformational leadership will thereby inspire the employees into confidence, loyalty, and respect in relation to their leaders, and they are motivated to do more than what they originally were willing to do (Bass, 1985). The employees are transformed by, first of all, being made aware of the importance and significance of the objectives that are being realized. Second, they are motivated to suppress their own interest for the benefit of the organization or the team. Finally, they are transformed when their need for self-realization is activated.

The underlying process of influence is unclear; however, it is possible to find some central factors based on reasoning (Yukl, 2006). Firstly, influence builds on the internalization of values. The goal is for the employees to develop and stand for the same values as the leader. This causes them to become emotionally attached to the values, and the values become an important basis for their motivation. Secondly, transformational leadership conditions a stronger sense of identification with the organization. This means that employees increasingly feel in harmony with the job, and they experience their own values as being the same as the organization's values. Ultimately, this leadership model causes the employees to feel a greater sense of achievement, both as individuals and as a group. To a greater extent, in other words, they find themselves able to handle the job requirements. Robust self-efficacy provides endurance in problem-solving and improves learning (Bandura, 1986).

Transactional leadership

A central aspect in transactional leadership is the contract between the leader and the employees, which aims to satisfy both employees and the organization's interests. The focus is, in other words, on the transactions between the organization and its employees. Employees will contribute their time, expertise, and motivation, and in return they receive salaries, a work environment, and tasks. The transactions therefore benefit both parties. The results of transactional leadership are often articulated in a labour contract, where the employee's work and remuneration are often specified.

Transactional leadership has two key elements (Bass & Avolio, 1993):

1. *Contingent reward*. This means that the rewards to the employees are conditioned by their efforts. In other words, a reciprocal transaction acts as a basis for the leadership exercised.
2. *Leadership by exception*. This means that the leadership will be activated when there is a deviation from what is agreed upon. If, for example, an "agreement" on how many cases to solve is established between a police chief and a police captain, the police chief will take action the moment the goal is not met. A distinction is made between an active form and a passive

form of this element. In the active form, leaders will engage strongly in the whole process and intervene if necessary. In the passive form, leaders will only intervene when there is a problem that ends up at the "leader's desk."

We see that this form of leadership differs from what is characterized as transformational leadership. In the last 30 years, transactional leadership has gained increasing importance within the public sector, with its emphasis on measurable results and formal contracts. In addition, a number of incentives are established. For example, a university will receive resources based upon the number of student credits being produced and the number of research papers published.

Laissez-faire leadership

This is a form of leadership whereby the leader barely interferes with what the employees are doing. To a large degree, laissez-faire leadership encourages an active use of self-leadership but without the follow-up of value-based leadership. This model of leadership is either based on indifference or on an understanding that employees do not need any leadership impulses.

By combining these three forms of leadership, a full-spectrum model emerges (Full Range of Leadership – Avolio & Bass, 1991) – a model that makes it possible to identify active and effective leadership behaviour. Here, these three forms of leadership are not presented as exclusive in relation to each other, suggesting that they can be combined and tailored to the individual situation. A leader can therefore exert transformational leadership, transactional leadership, and laissez-faire leadership. The composition can vary over time and may be dependent on the specific situation. At the same time, the model assumes that transformational leadership is the most active and effective leadership model.

Yet the theory of transformational leadership is also criticized (for reviews, see Andersen, 2011; Yukl, 2006). Among other things, it is argued that the theory has a weak leadership basis. It does not adequately specify how employees are affected, and there is too little focus on the organization's objectives. How will this theory score when compared to our definition of value-based leadership? To answer this question, we will take a look at the various dimensions.

Anchored on high ethical standards

Transformational leadership is clearly anchored on high ethical principles (Bass & Steidelmeier, 1999). Emphasis is placed on both the leader's moral character and the ethical basis for the leader's values. It is also indicated that authentic leadership should be exercised, meaning that the leader's behaviour must be real, with a clear link to the leader's personal values.

Anchored on the organization's values

Being anchored on the organization's values is more obscure to some extent, although it is described in the original definition (Burns, 1978) where employee awareness of these values should be promoted. When it comes to anchoring the values, a stronger emphasis is placed on leader's values than on the organization's values (MacTavish & Kolb, 2008), pointing to the assumption that the leader's values are internalized by employees.

Development of the organization's values

As mentioned above, the emphasis is on employee internalization of the leader's values. Thus, a developmental perspective is present, but it is not a prominent part of the theory.

Anchored on the leadership process

The theory of transformational leadership does not have an explicit focus on the leadership process. This means that there is not a large focus on leadership being an intentional process conducted by a person to manage the activities and relations within a group or organization. However implicit, we can to a certain extent say that the leadership process is present.

In summary, transformational leadership does not completely meet the previously established criteria for the concept of value-based leadership. However, as we can note, there are relatively large similarities. Based on this, we choose to present a model which integrates the key elements in the theory of transformational leadership with our definition of value-based leadership (see Figure 10.1).

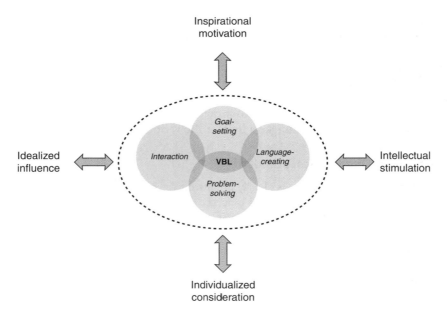

Figure 10.1 Transformational leadership in a value and leadership-based perspective

The model in Figure 10.1 shows that transformational leadership should have a clear value-based perspective. First, the leadership that is practised must build on high ethical standards. Second, the leadership must be firmly anchored in the organization's values. Within highly professional organizations, this means that the profession's values must be the basis for the transformational leadership. It is not enough that the leader wants to see the employees internalize his values. Research has shown that it is very difficult to transfer the leader's values to the employees (Brown, 2002, cited in MacTavish & Kolb, 2008). Finally, there should be a definite value-development perspective in transformational leadership. The values present in an organization must be developed so that they are in line with task requirements and the organization's surroundings.

The model also indicates that transformational leadership should be drawn from a clear leadership perspective. Based on the applied model, this implies that leadership must focus both on the development of objectives and how these objectives are to be realized. Thus, transformational leadership must capture both the goal-setting and problem-solving processes. In other words, there must be an overarching goal for why employees need to be transformed to higher ethical standards and motivational levels. The motivation must also be directed towards realizing the organization's key objectives.

Finally, the model captures the "four I's" in transformational leadership: idealized influence, inspirational motivation, intellectual stimulation, and individual consideration. These dimensions are what identify transformational leadership as a distinct form of value-based leadership.

10.2   Elements of transformational leadership

As shown in the previous section, the main dimensions of transformational leadership are idealized influence, inspirational motivation, intellectual stimulation, and individual consideration. Transformational leadership thereby emerges as a more distinct concept. Let us now take a closer look at what these four dimensions entail.

Idealized influence

This is a leadership behaviour leading to the creation of a strong emotional relationship between the leader and the employees – something that contributes to the employees identifying with the leader. Idealized influence is also associated with charismatic leadership. This is a leadership form that has a lot of similarities with transformational leadership. Charisma is a Greek word which means "spiritual gifts" in the context of producing miracles and anticipating future events. There are currently several theories of charismatic leadership. One of them assumes that charismatic leaders basically do not have any special charismatic qualities. Instead, the charismatic qualities are assigned to the leaders when employees observe their behaviour (Conger & Kanungo, 1998). Examples of such behaviour include leaders having extreme visions, taking great personal risk, using unconventional strategies, and resorting to personal power to influence employees. Leaders practising behaviours like these are interpreted as charismatic – they are, in other words, given charismatic properties. In these situations, employees will identify with their leader, and they will in turn work hard to attain the leader's visions and goals.

In further developments of these theories, stress has been placed on the relationship between leaders and employees (Shamir et al., 1993). It is also assumed that leaders are endowed with extraordinary abilities; however, this is not a necessary condition for exercising charismatic leadership. Among others, important behavioural features of such leaders are that they:

- express an attractive vision
- use strong emotional means to communicate their vision
- take personal risks and sacrifice themselves in order to realize the vision
- communicate high expectations
- express confidence in employees
- identify themselves with the group or the organization
- are committed to empowering employees.

In other words, leaders who practise this form of behaviour will be perceived as charismatic. An important condition is that the leaders express a vision which is consistent with the values and identity of the employees. This means that in a highly professional organization, the visions must be thoroughly integrated with the profession's values and identity. This form of leadership entices the employees to identify strongly with both the leadership and the organization. In addition, employees will develop a stronger sense of efficacy – both individually and as a group. Together, this will create a behaviour which is directed towards realizing the leaders' visions.

Idealized influence is a very important part of transformational leadership, and here the value perspective is particularly evident. The leaders must be anchored on a solid value and have overt visions that contribute to a strong feeling of affiliation with the organization. Furthermore, relations of trust between leaders and employees are important – and, among other things, are created by common goals and values.

Inspirational motivation

The second dimension of transformational leadership is inspirational motivation. This is also closely linked to charismatic leadership and indicates that the leader must motivate employees to work towards the overall goals and visions. It is, among other things, important that the leader acts as a good role model. It must be obvious that the leader is motivated in relation to the visions that are developed. Employees will observe the leader's energy, commitment, and behaviour regarding the vision. They will also register what rewards the leader

receives – perhaps the excitement gained from challenges, the opportunities arising from learning, or the recognition and strong satisfaction derived from the
work. In so doing, employees are encouraged to copy the behaviour through
model-learning. And in this they may unconsciously be searching for the same
rewards or stronger identification with a leader whom they admire.

By divulging his or her visions, a leader can communicate the overall purpose
of the job and put it into a larger context. The employees see that they are part
of a larger picture and then see the job as more meaningful. For a teacher, the
focus can shift from simply teaching students the English language, to educat-
ing and socializing future generations. Similarly, a police officer's work may be
envisaged as providing security for the community, which may be more meaningful when compared to describing the work as merely enforcing drinking and
driving laws.

This is not necessarily an easy process. For most people, small and large challenges characterize everyday life, and it can be difficult to stop and look around.
Visions can be perceived as platitudes that nobody cares about. Therefore, it is
necessary to have communication skills; that is, the leader must be able to communicate the vision in a way that captivates employees. Emotion and energy
must be created within an organization, and key values must be enabled, which
is why crisis periods are important (but not necessary) conditions for charismatic
leadership (Shamir et al., 1993). When an organization's existence is at stake
or is threatened, strong feelings arise, and extraordinary efforts are legitimized.
These are ideal conditions for transformational leadership, where the overarching goals are clear and where employees are more easily inspired into action.

Intellectual stimulation

While intellectual challenges are crucial elements in times of transformation,
intellectual stimulation is often given inadequate attention when thinking about
transformational leadership (Bass, 2008). Transformational leadership is not
only directed towards emotions, but it should also be directed towards the intellect. While this does not suggest that leaders have to possess certain intellectual abilities, it does point to the importance of being able to stimulate the
intellect of others – facilitating curiosity, developing creativity, and finding new
approaches.

Intellectual stimulation can also be linked to motivation by the employees
being given the opportunity to realize their capabilities. They are given major
challenges and must stretch to solve new problems. Thus, they will meet their
needs for growth (Alderfer, 1972), which among other things are related to personal development. In addition to creating motivation through communication
of visions (inspirational motivation), transformational leadership will also help
facilitate motivation by creating challenging assignments.

The most important intellectual stimulation is to make a creative and
highly adaptable environment. This requires emphasizing self-leadership and

empowerment. In order to release energy and find new solutions, employees must be given the freedom to act. They must have the opportunity to break new grounds. The leader will serve as an inspirer who asks questions and challenges employees to look at things from new perspectives. In the process, it becomes possible to avoid conventional thinking and stimulate double-loop learning. Employees must reflect on whether their own values and patterns of behaviour are still functional. In a busy and chaotic day at work, the leader can create a new focus or create a new structure which opens up for new insights.

At a university, for example, a dean can ask whether it is still necessary to lecture, thereby challenging employees to find new ways to disseminate research results to the academic community or to students. Or at an elementary school, the principal may ask if any of the programmes designed to prevent bullying really have an effect, or whether there are other ways to approach this problem. Leaders must, in other words, challenge the organization's established "truths" – truths that can often block innovation and renewal.

Individualized consideration

The last dimension is individualized consideration. The leader must "see" the individual employee. A supportive climate should be developed, and focus should be placed on the individual's need for personal development. We can say that the leader will act as a mentor and a coach – being a good conversation partner and encouraging learning and development. Delegation and self-leadership are also important here. The individual will be given new assignments based on maturity and professional development. Employees are not a group, but a collection of individuals with personal needs, aspirations, and opportunities.

We can also say that this represents a dimension of care with an emphasis on establishing personal relations. This can be as simple as the leader remembering names, family situations, and other personal information about employees, or perhaps what they talked about last time they met. This means that the leader must be an active listener and have a real interest in the employees' concerns. Another important consideration is to treat employees with respect. Criticism should be constructive and be provided in a way that promotes learning and development.

These four dimensions show that transformational leadership is an extensive concept. A leader will to a varying degree score highly on all dimensions. It is important to see that the theory is also consistent with transaction leadership and laissez-faire leadership. Leadership is complex and does not always have a simple answer. Each leader must find a form that works best. If we are to use the term *value-based leadership behaviour*, a clear focus must be placed on goal-setting and problem-solving, preferably combined with language development and interaction. And if we use the term *value-based leadership*, we must have a clear value anchor.

Example 16

The Danish Immigration Service

The Danish Immigration Service in 2006 began a transformation from a civil service bureaucracy to a service provider. It had been an organization with a strong negative image and subject to much media criticism. It had low user satisfaction with NGOs (non-governmental organizations) making many complaints. However, the official government policy was to tighten up on immigration.

The change required transformational leadership, especially from the CEO and top management team. This included a major value change associated with a new vision for the organization, the development of a customer focus, and the introduction of LEAN-style systems. The success of the change was associated with strong leadership and engaging the workforce as a whole in the project. The change encouraged, generated, and utilized user feedback and suggestion – something previously not part of the ethos of the Service.

10.3   Developing visions

As we have learned, visions are an important part of transformational leadership. We will therefore look more closely at what this term involves. It is first important to state that visions should have a solid value base, which increases the possibility that they provide both an emotional and a motivational effect. These are necessary if the vision is to work well in a leadership context. It should capture the core values and build bridges between past, present, and future. Thus, it will represent meaningful future goals. We can set a few basic demands for what characterizes a good vision (Bass, 2008). It should:

- highlight the purpose of the business
- create meaning
- create emotion and motivation
- be intellectually stimulating
- communicate complex ideas in a simple way
- represent an optimistic view of the future.

These are heavy demands that are naturally hard to meet. At the same time, they provide important criteria for evaluating visions. To what extent will a concrete vision live up to these? The most famous vision is perhaps John F. Kennedy's when on 25 May 1961 he said that the United States would have a man on the moon within ten years. The vision was realized in the summer of 1969. This vision gave clear direction: It created meaning for the whole nation, pride, and positive feelings; it was an intellectual stimulant, and optimistically conveyed a high level of complexity. The use of visions in the context of leadership can be traced back to the 1980s (Conger, 2000). Since then, visions have been actively used in both private and public organizations.

Example 17

Martin Luther King

The leadership vision demonstrated by Dr Martin Luther King is encapsulated in his famous "I have a dream speech" which is quoted in part below. The speech demonstrates the espousal of a fundamental value system, which King derived in part from the fundamental values of America itself as embedded in its constitution that man is created free and equal. The training that King received as a preacher enabled him to evoke a power in communication through the mechanism of repeating "I have a dream" and also through the actual mechanism of delivery with the skilful use of slow presentation and pauses. The power of the words in conveying a set of fundamental ethical values is still as valid today as when it was delivered. Perhaps significantly, the words were not part of the original speech King had prepared for delivery but rather were an inspirational inclusion. The "I have a dream" had been delivered by him in speeches on previous but lesser occasions, and several members of the audience called out to him to repeat it. King recognized that it was right for the occasion and history has proven him right.

"And so even though we face the difficulties of today and tomorrow, I still have a dream. It is a dream deeply rooted in the American dream. I have a dream that one day this nation will rise up and live out the true meaning of its creed: 'We hold these truths to be self-evident, that all men are created equal.' I have a dream that one day on the red hills of Georgia, the sons of former slaves and the sons of former slave owners will be able to sit down together at the table of brotherhood. I have a dream that one day even the state of Mississippi, a state sweltering with the heat of injustice, sweltering with the heat of oppression, will be transformed into an oasis of freedom and justice. I have a dream that my four little children will one day live in a nation where they will not be judged by the colour of their skin but by the content of their character."

We have in this book assumed that visions are used internally in relation to value-based leadership. However, visions also have an important external function. They provide a picture of the organization and can contribute to creating a good reputation and a high sense of legitimacy. In this respect, it is very important that visions are short and easy to communicate; for example, Nokia's "Connecting people." For a vision to work both internally and externally, we can formulate the following requirements (Hatch & Schultz, 2008). It must be firmly anchored on:

- the organization's culture
- the organization's identity
- the environment's perceived image of the organization.

We see that the last requirement is directed towards external conditions. It indicates that the vision to a certain extent must be consistent with the already formed image of the organization in its environment. If the gap between vision and image is too large, the vision can easily be perceived as false and an attempt at embellishment. This can have an opposite effect and undermine the organization's reputation.

The first two requirements have an internal focus. Vision must encompass both values and identity, and if we implement this into a highly professional organization, we can argue that the vision must be anchored on both the profession's culture and its identity. In addition to the vision being in line with fundamental professional values, it must also symbolize "who we are." It must provide a symbolic expression of "our" perceived identity. This is without doubt a daunting exercise – one that cannot adequately be expressed through a short slogan. One option then is to use more words to describe the vision. An example from a public nursing home reads as follows:

"Focusing on what is in the best interests of patients and society, Øya Community Hospital shall develop good and comprehensive care and treatment programmes across administration levels, education levels and professions." (Øya Community Hospital, http://www.trondheim. kommune.no/content/1117729400/Oya-helsehus---Information-in-english, November 18, 2013)

Instead of searching for a short formulation, they have chosen to use one longer sentence. Longer formulations are more comprehensive and precise, but are also more difficult to communicate – especially in relation to external stakeholders. Another advantage with short formulations is that they provide more room for different interpretations. Thus, they may have a longer lifetime. They may be reinterpreted as the situation changes.

The greatest challenge with visions is that they can be seen as simply "hanging in the air;" that is, the leaders' concoction of empty words that no one really cares about. They become too general and fail to create emotion, motivation, and commitment. Two requirements can be made in order to deal with this (Johnsen, 2002). The vision must:

- be tied to a clear commitment
- be consistent – on the organizational level – with the employees' personal visions.

To analyse these requirements, Johnsen has developed a model with four elements:

1. *Ideal State.* This is the organization's general vision.
2. *Programme Statement.* This is a formal statement at the organizational level to work towards the vision.
3. *Lodestar.* This is each employee's personal vision.
4. *Specific Aspirations.* This is the individual employee's commitment to work towards his or her own vision.

First, the individual's vision (lodestar) must be in line with the organization's vision (ideal state). If the organization's vision is clearly anchored on the profession's culture and identity, then there is a higher probability that the link between the individual and the organization will be strong. If the individual's wishes and dreams about personal development are not in sync with the organization's vision, it is unlikely that the general vision will have any effect on employee's behaviour. When this is the case, it will be difficult to perform any kind of transformational leadership.

Second, both the ideal state and the lodestar must be linked to specific commitments. It is not enough to have a vision. There must also be willingness and commitment aimed at realizing the vision – both at the organizational level and at the employee level. When the Furu Steiner School articulates the vision "We create enthusiasm for learning," it must simultaneously adopt a binding plan of action which shows how to realize the vision. And the individual teacher must find his or her own vision aimed at creating enthusiasm among students. The teacher needs to have clear aspirations for how this vision will be realized.

If all the visions in an organization have a good value base, are thoroughly integrated with each other, and linked together by clear commitments, it is easier to use visions as an active part of developing transformational leadership.

10.4 Summary

Transformational leadership is a key form of leadership which is particularly important when there arises a need to engage in major organizational change based on higher-order values. The origins lie in part within writing about political leadership (Burns, 1978). It can be contracted with transactional leadership and represents a value-based leadership on the organizational level. Drawing on Burns, further theories of transformational leadership have identified components including idealized influence, inspirational motivation, intellectual stimulation, and individualized consideration.

Transactional leadership possesses a central aspect relating to the contract between the leader and staff which aims to meet the interests of both. It has the elements of contingent reward and leadership by exception. It has gained increasing influence over recent years.

Laissez-faire leadership – where the leader barely interferes – provides a third concept of leadership, and the three types of leadership can combine to form a spectrum (Avolio & Bass, 1991). The theoretical and research base for transformational leadership have been criticized by some as not strong enough (Yukl, 2006). However, it is important to understand its dimensions and the importance of the value base. In particular, transformational leadership typically involves the development of a vision by the leader. The vision must both be possessed by the leader and owned by the organization itself. This chapter has set out the nature of what would constitute a good vision, noting that this is hard to achieve. Martin Luther King perhaps furnishes such an example. In organizational terms an individuals vision needs to be consistent with that of their organization. Johnsen's model is set out with four elements of an ideal state, a programme statement, a lodestar, and specific aspirations.

Exercises for further development and understanding

- How might you explain transformational leadership to a group of colleagues who are used to a conventional bureaucracy? Why and how might it be different to what they have experienced?
- Consider a situation in your experience where an organization was in crisis and a new leader was brought in to turn the organization around. What did the new leader do to achieve this? Do you recognize any of the characteristics of transformational leadership in what the person did? If the person failed, then where might they have done things differently?
- Why are values important in transformational leadership? Consider a situation where there is a need for a major change which is largely technical in nature (such as computerizing an organization which previously relied on paper-based systems). Why would a values base be important here?

Recommended further reading

Bass, M.B. (2008). *The Bass Handbook of Leadership*. New York: Free Press.

Value-based leadership – some conclusions

11

Key learning points

At the end of this chapter the reader should:

- be aware of the three major perspectives of value-based leadership
- understand why a distinct leadership theory is needed to understand the concept of value-based leadership
- be aware of the major value dimensions that are needed in a theory of value-based leadership
- understand the mix of governance forms that exist in the public sector
- comprehend how value-based leadership on different levels are integrated in an organizational setting.

Public professions are a cornerstone in today's welfare society. They are responsible for the production of public services and symbolize important values in society. Traditionally, public professions have had the freedom to decide how to carry out their jobs and how the services in their profession should be organized. This sovereignty has been challenged by the rise of New Public Management (NPM). New performance measurement systems have been introduced; the focus is now placed on measurable results, and various forms of competition have been implemented. In our opinion, this development must be balanced by a stronger focus on values, identity, belonging, and commitment among professional employees. Value-based leadership in this context is an interesting concept that gives consideration to both the politician's need for sound leadership and the profession's need for developing high-quality services. In Chapter 1 we introduced three perspectives of value-based leadership: a leadership perspective, a value perspective, and a public perspective. Before we conclude by summarizing with an integrated value-based leadership model, we will take a closer look at these three perspectives.

11.1   The leadership perspective

The most fundamental dimension in this book is leadership. Without a clear leadership focus, value-based leadership loses its foundation. Therefore, we have to ask the question: What is leadership? As demonstrated in Chapter 5, there is no clear answer to this question. Different theories emphasize different dimensions of the leadership concept.

This does not necessarily mean that some leadership theories are right and others are wrong. All theories provide insights, and theory diversity shows that leadership is a complex phenomenon. The fundamental core of most leadership theories is that leadership is an intentional process directed towards preparing and realizing organizational goals (Yukl, 2006). This fundamental core is valid across a variety of settings. A student must exercise leadership when developing his or her career, a teacher must exercise leadership when creating a good class environment, and a hospital director must exercise leadership to develop a well-functioning hospital. Everyone must have some goals to work towards, and everyone must find an appropriate way to achieve the goals.

Although this is the basis for most of the leadership theories, there is quite a difference between them. Some theories emphasize the leader's personal characteristics, some emphasize the leader's behaviour, some emphasize that leadership must be adjusted to the situation, and some emphasize the leader–employee relationship. It is therefore important to search for a fruitful theory – one that can be applied in practical situations and that supports solving the organization's fundamental challenges to goal achievement.

To find a leadership theory that is suitable for developing the concept of value-based leadership in the professions of public administration, we must start with what characterizes these organizations. We have chosen to place particular emphasis on two aspects. First, professional employees have a high degree of expertise and a great deal of freedom in how to conduct their work. This indicates that the search should be for a leadership theory which assumes that leadership can be performed by all employees in the organization. Leadership behaviour of formal leaders is important; however, it must be balanced against all the decisions taken by professional employees. Every day, doctors, nurses, social workers, teachers, and other professionals must prioritize different goals and find solutions to complex challenges in order to create high quality and efficiency. There is a need for a leadership theory that highlights these efforts and makes it possible to make both formal leaders and professional employees accountable.

Second, professional workers are motivated by personal growth, autonomy, and quality (Tampoe, 1993). Based on this, it is important to have a leadership theory that has a strong focus on interaction, both vertically and horizontally. If we assume that employees are genuinely committed to creating high quality, there is less need for control and more need for collaboration.

Based on these two characteristics, relevant theories are limited. In particular, there are a few theories that allow for both managers and employees to exercise leadership. Most leadership theories explicitly or implicitly assume that leadership is exercised by formal leaders. We have, therefore, chosen to place the main emphasis on a leadership theory that focuses on leadership processes rather than the behaviour of formal leaders (Johnsen, 2006). It is open for everyone to participate in the leadership processes. At a school, this may be a principal, a teacher, a student who sits in the student council, or a parent who engages in the development of the school. The theory contains four key dimensions, where leadership is defined as a goal-setting, problem-solving, and language-creating interaction.

The theory is simple and yet complex at the same time. The four dimensions are meaningful in all social contexts and can be used as a compass to measure leadership quality. To what extent are managers and employees aware of the organization's central goals? How strong is the organization's focus on creating better results? Is the organization working continuously on enhancements, or must it be pressured to do so by its stakeholders? Has the organization developed a language and acquired the expertise necessary to formulate good objectives and find good solutions? Finally, how do the interactions in the organization function – between the organization and its stakeholders, between managers and employees, and between people at the same organizational level?

These are simple yet essential questions for assessing how well leadership functions. At the same time, this leadership theory is highly complex, where it is possible to distinguish between different goals, problem-solving techniques, languages, and forms of interaction. These elements can be entered into matrices that provide a more complex picture of the leadership process. If these analyses are made at several organizational levels, a complex pattern emerges which illustrates how individuals, departments, and the total system function with regard to leadership. High complexity is not an end itself, but it is important that the theory, if desired, can be used for more in-depth analysis of the organization's leadership processes.

11.2   The value perspective

The second perspective of this book is the concept of value. What is value? How are values developed? How can we articulate the organization's values? On this dimension, the theories are more consistent – at least at a basic level. This does not mean that the theories are simple. Indeed, the complexity is high, and there is a wealth of literature that analyses various dimensions within the concept.

Since goal-setting and problem-solving are two core elements in the leadership concept, we have chosen to include a theory which distinguishes between terminal and instrumental values (Rokeach, 1976). While terminal values represent desirable final states, instrumental values indicate which action is preferable. Thus, this theory is highly relevant in the context of leadership. Terminal values can function as criteria for prioritizing various objectives, while instrumental values can be used to regulate which methods should be used to realize the objectives.

When the values are being integrated with a leadership theory, their effect on human behaviour is an important characteristic. To capture this, we have implemented a theory that emphasizes the value's cognitive, emotional, and motivational elements (Kluckhohn, 1951). For values to influence behaviour, the last two elements are especially important. It is not enough to talk about values. The values must also have a strong emotional attachment. In other words, behaviour that is consistent with the values creates positive emotions, while behaviour that violates the values creates negative emotions. This affects one's own behaviour as well as the behaviour of others. Moreover, the values must have a strong motivational basis, where a strong inner drive aims at complying with the values. If these two elements are present, the values are internalized – they have become an integrated part of the personality and will to a large extent affect actual behaviour. In a leadership context, it is important to work with all three elements.

Previously, we have demonstrated that the public sector is characterized by various ways of thinking. Different logics are practised side by side, creating major leadership challenges (Fjellvær, 2010). To capture this, we have integrated theories that shed light on value-related conflicts. The values can occur in clusters, where one central value is linked with a number of other values (Beck-Jørgensen, 2003a, 2006). Thus, we can get a professional cluster, an economic cluster, and a bureaucratic cluster – three different sets of values that may be in conflict with each other. This provides an important insight for understanding the challenges associated with value-based leadership in public professions.

Although in principle the values exist only at the individual level, it is useful to talk about values at a group level. This does not mean that all individuals in the group have identical values, but a portion of their values are shared. This can be anything from small groups of friends to large nations. We have in this book emphasized professional culture. There is a common set of values that over time has evolved within the various professions. Insight into the culture of one's own profession is necessary if one is to work with value-based leadership in this profession. This necessity is not only important so that leadership can have a solid grounding in professional values, but so that leadership can renew the profession by challenging its traditional culture.

11.3   The public perspective

Leadership in public institutions is always influenced by the public context. Especially important are the various forms of governance that have evolved. These forms are the frameworks for the discretion that public employees have in their jobs, and provide clear guidelines for decision making. In order to understand the dilemmas associated with value-based leadership, it is important to have an insight into the managerial changes that have taken place over the last 30 years.

These changes are clarified when distinguishing between four forms of governance: hierarchical, market, network, and clan (Beck-Jørgensen & Vrangbæk, 2004; Thompson, 2001). These are systems that have been established to coordinate human activity. They are present in public organizations and influence the leadership processes that take place. The kind of value-based leadership that can be developed is largely dependent on the combination of governance forms that are utilized within each organization.

The main characteristic of *hierarchical* governance is the presence of several leadership levels within the organization. This is a well-tested organizational form which for the most part has been a success. The control mechanisms within the hierarchy are plentiful. Firstly, employees must submit to an authority which enables order to be achieved. Secondly, both managers and employees have a defined area of authority and responsibility. The area of authority determines what decisions they can make, and area of responsibility specifies which tasks should be performed and what results should be obtained. Finally, a set of bureaucratic rules regulates the behaviour of all employees. This includes everything from when and where to work, to how the work should be performed.

Market-type governance is based on independent actors regulating each other through competition. This is a dominant form of governance within the private sector, where companies are governed by market competition. Retaining customers requires companies to continuously strive to develop products and services with a competitive edge. The market's control mechanism derives from consumers comparing organizations, products, and services, where the price and quality serve as the basis for consumers' particular choices.

Clan-type governance is based on the development of a set of common values and in all social groups. These values regulate human behaviour in two ways. First, values will, over time, be internalized by group members. These members will inherit the values as their own, thus giving way to a powerful form of self-regulation. Second, a form of social control will also develop. Group members will adapt to the dominant values established in the group to avoid social sanctions. In public institutions, both professional and organizational cultures have these features.

Finally, *network*-type governance builds on the fact that all organizations face challenges that are difficult to handle alone. Therefore, they establish co-operative relationships with other organizations that can complement their expertise and capacity. An example of this is that in order to solve drug problems among children and adolescents, the police, schools, and child welfare services must work together. The governance element of the networks is the agreements (formal and informal) entered into between the partners and the trust that develops between the people who interact in the network.

Traditionally, the two main forms of public-sector governance have been hierarchical and clan forms. Hierarchical types have been dominant within public administration and are present in the form of a government bureaucracy. This has been necessary for ensuring a successful implementation of policy decisions and safeguarding values such as neutrality, equality, and justice. The clan has, in turn, been dominant in service production – that is, within the public-sector professions. This has been necessary to ensure good governance in a situation characterized by high complexity, low standardized tasks, and a great deal of freedom in work execution.

(NPM) has resulted in a shift between these four forms of governance. First, the market type has gained an increased significance through the introduction of competition between public organizations. This development was made possible through new systems for performance measurement. Being able to measure results in a satisfactory manner also makes it possible to make comparisons. Thus, this provides a basis for obtaining competitive bids or assigning resources based on results obtained. The worst performance is punished while the best is rewarded.

Increased use of market-type solutions has reduced the element of both hierarchical governance and clan governance. In the hierarchy, there is more decentralization with greater discretion for lower-level managers. The clan has lost its significance due to the increasing use of performance indicators. Previously, professionals assessed each other's quality (peer control); now formal performance measures are being conducted as a basis for how institutions should be organized and managed. Meanwhile, the clan has become more bureaucratized. When compared to the past, rules and formal procedures are more often used to govern professional employees today. The result of this is that the regulatory role of values is reduced in public professions.

An additional change is that networks have become more important. Increasing decentralization has resulted in the emergence of a polycentric society (Sand, 2004); that is, a society with several independent centres of activity. This makes it difficult to manage problems that are interdisciplinary and cross-sectoral in nature – the so-called "wicked problems" (Grint, 2010). These problems are characterized by a high level of complexity, with no easy solution and no clear connection between cause and effect. They are very difficult to handle and typically require collaboration across independent institutions. An example is the development of the national healthcare system, which entails complex problems like the location of hospitals, the role of front-line services, the particular authority that should be delegated to each healthcare institution, the diseases or patient groups that should be prioritized, and the approach for leading various healthcare professions. There are no elegant solutions – dilemmas, paradoxes, and complexities lead to an acceptance of what Grint (2001) calls "clumsy solutions." These problems are too complex to be resolved within one agency or one organization. Instead, a network which can collectively find acceptable solutions must be established.

Initially, value-based leadership could be integrated with all governance types. The hierarchy, market, clan, and network all build on a fundamental set of values. In this book we have chosen to focus on value-based leadership in public professions, which points to clan-type governance and the importance of professional values. As the same time, the trend indicates that more value clusters eventually manifest themselves in public professions. The hierarchy, market, and network have all gained a stronger position, and this creates major leadership challenges in professional organizations. These dilemmas cannot be removed easily. Currently, all four forms of governance are necessary in the public sector, which requires value-based leadership to balance different logics and different values. Value-based leadership is therefore not an easy solution that creates harmony and removes value conflicts. Nonetheless, it represents a form of leadership that makes it possible to highlight the clan's significance in professional organizations. It will thus appear as an important option which can complement other forms of governance and leadership.

11.4   An integrated model of value-based leadership

The purpose of this book has not been to develop a new leadership theory. Our desire has been to put the leadership processes that take place in public professions into a value perspective. Based on this, we have defined value-based leadership as "a goal-setting, problem-solving, language-creating, and value-developing interaction which is anchored on the organization's values and high ethical standards. Value-based leadership can be exercised at the individual level, group level, and organizational level." In other words, the concept of value has been integrated with an existing leadership theory. First, we have focused on three factors:

1. Leadership processes must be anchored on the values that are present in the organization.
2. Leadership processes must be based on high ethical standards.
3. Leadership processes must be aimed at creating functional values.

The first factor indicates that leadership of public professions must be anchored on the present professional and organizational cultures; leadership must therefore not be in conflict with the organization's basic values. This congruence is not that simple, as conflicting values are present in most organizations. Both employees and managers will, therefore, experience many dilemmas related to practising value-based leadership.

The second factor indicates that leadership must be based on the ethical standards present in the organization's environment, which means that the organization must comply with the expectations of the surrounding society. This is especially important for public institutions. Maintaining a good reputation depends on the institutions being seen as carriers of society's fundamental values.

The last factor indicates that the values are always in motion and that leaders are responsible for developing functional values that are in harmony with society's values. This means that all employees have to be thoroughly aware of how an organization's basic values change. Developing values is a demanding process, and the question of which values are desirable and which values should be adjusted needs to be asked.

Based on the selected leadership model, we have further stated that all dimensions of the leadership concept must have a strong foundation of values. This means as follows:

- the goals must be consistent with the organization's terminal values
- the problem-solving methods must be consistent with the organization's instrumental values
- a language must be developed that makes it possible to work with the values of the organization
- values that promote good relationships within the organization must be developed.

At this level, it is easier to evaluate whether or not the leadership behaviour is value-based, and if there is need for adjustments. Challenges, dilemmas, and conflicts also become more visible, which can form a solid basis for processes aimed at adjustments of both behaviour and values.

Our definition of value-based leadership also allows for this model to be exercised at various organizational levels. This means, first and foremost, that all employees must take responsibility for ensuring that their own leadership behaviour has a solid footing in values, which is very important in public professions. We have referred to this as self-leadership. All employees who have authority to make decisions will exercise leadership – whether they are aware of this or not. By incorporating self-leadership, value-based leadership becomes a concept that is thoroughly adapted to heavily professional organizations. Employees must be accountable for which objectives they are working towards and which methods they employ to create good results. And they will have to reflect on the extent to which their behaviour has a solid basis in the organization's values and ethical standards.

Second, leadership will be exercised in all social situations where groups of employees – such as management teams, project teams, workgroups, or other types of groups – meet to discuss challenges related to objectives and results. Relationships are brought closer together, and it is important to be aware of which values are developed in the process. Teams have a shared responsibility for creating good results and will not function properly without a common value platform.

Finally, value-based leadership can be exercised by formal departmental or institutional leaders. Through their status, these leaders have a large influence within the organization. They emerge as important role models and provide, through their behaviour, strong signals on which values are given priority in real terms. They also symbolize the organization externally and affect both credibility and legitimacy. We have chosen to take a closer look at transformational leadership that emphasizes several important aspects of the relationship between manager and employee.

Value-based leadership at various levels should be integrated. The values symbolized by formal leaders should be reflected in the values that are developed at the group level, and at the same time the values developed at the group level should affect the set of values for formal leaders. In the same way, the values developed in dense communities (groups and teams) affect – and are affected by – individual values.

As Figure 11.1 illustrates, value-based leadership is placed within a public, a professional, and a societal context. This means firstly that the values forming the basis for leadership in public professions must be in line with the core values of the public. A good correlation will help the organization achieve political acceptance – which helps to ensure future access to resources. Secondly, the values must be in line with the overall values in relevant professions. This will ensure that professional organizations can maintain their role with regard to further development of the profession's formal value basis. Finally, the values must be in line with the core social values, which will contribute to the organization's high level of legitimacy in society. The organization becomes institutionalized and emerges as an important carrier of the society's values.

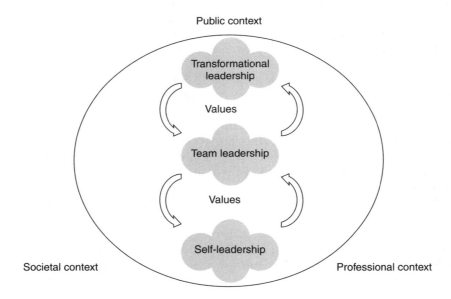

Figure 11.1   An integrated model of value-based leadership

Exercises for further development and understanding

- In this book we have used a process-oriented leadership theory to develop a concept for values-based leadership. An alternative is to use a theory that is based on the personal attributes of the leaders. Discuss the strengths and weaknesses of these two alternatives.

- What is in your opinion the most important part of the value concept?
- Picture an organization that you are familiar with. Describe the different governance forms (hierarchy, market, clan, network) that exist in the organization and discuss the value conflicts that may occur if a stronger value-based leadership based on clan values is introduced in the organization.
- Discuss the challenges that may occur if an organization tries to establish the same values in the leadership process on all levels of the organization.

References

Aadland, E. (2011). The ethical reflection process. In Aaland, E. & Matulayová, T. (eds), *Ethical reflection in the helping professions*. Prešov: University of Prešov.

Abbott, A. (1988). *The system of professions*. Chicago: The University of Chicago Press.

Albert, S. & Whetten, D.A. (1985). Organizational identity. I L.L. Cummings & B.M Staw (eds), *Research in organizational behaviour* (vol. 7, 263–95). Greenwich, CT: JAI Press.

Alderfer, C.P. (1972). *Existence, relatedness, and growth*. New York: Free Press.

Andersen, J. Aa. (2011). *Ledelsesteorier. Om ledelse skal lede til noe*. Bergen: Fagbokforlaget.

Argyris, C. (2001). *On organizational learning*. Oxford: Blackwell.

Argyris, C. & D. Schön (1978). *Organizational learning: A theory of action perspective*. Reading, MA: Addison Wesley.

Assmann, R. (ed.) (2008). *Teamorganisering. Veien til mer fleksible organisasjoner*. Bergen: Fagbokforlaget.

Avolio, B.J. & Bass, B.M. (1991). *Full range of leadership development*. Binghamton, NY: Bass, Avolio & Associates.

Avolio, B.J. & Gardner, W.L. (2005). Authentic leadership development: Getting to the root of positive forms of leadership. *The Leadership Quarterly*, 16, 315–338.

Bandura, A. (1986). *Social foundation of thought and action*. Englewood Cliffs, NJ: Prentice Hall.

Bang, H. (2008). Effektivitet i lederteam – hva er det, og hvilke faktorer påvirker det? *Tidsskrift for Norsk Psykologforening*, 3 (45), 272–286.

Bang, H. (2011). *Organisasjonskultur*. Oslo: Universitetsforlaget.

Barnard, C. (1938). *The function of the executive*. Cambridge, MA: Harvard University Press.

Bass, M.B. (1985). *Leadership and performance beyond expectation*. New York: Free Press.

Bass, M.B. (2008). *The Bass handbook of leadership*. New York: Free Press.

Bass, M.B. & Avolio, B.J. (1993). Transformational leadership: A response to critiques. In M.M. Chemers & R. Ayman (eds), *Leadership theory and research: Perspectives and directions* (49–80). New York: Free Press.

Bass, M.B. & Steidlmeier, P. (1999). Ethics, character, and authentic transformational leadership behavior. *The Leadership Quarterly*, 10 (2), 181–218.

Bauer, T.N., Morrison, E.W. & Callister, R.R. (1998). Organizational socialization: A review of directions for future research. In G.R. Ferris (ed.), *Research in personnel and human resources management* (vol. 16, 149–214). Greenwich, CT: JAI Press.

Beck-Jørgensen, T. (2003a). Konturene af en offentlig identitet. In Beck Jørgensen, T. (ed.), *På sporet af en offentlig identitet: værdier i stat, amter og kommuner* (240–260). Århus: Århus Universitetsforlag.

Beck-Jørgensen, T. (2003b). Værdier i harmoni, konflikt og forandring. In Beck-Jørgensen, T. (ed.), *På sporet af en offentlig identitet*. Århus: Århus Universitetsforlag.

Beck-Jørgensen, T. & Vrangbæk, K. (2004). Det offentlige styringsunivers. Fra government til governance? København: Maktudredningen.

Beck-Jørgensen, T. (2006). Value consciousness and public management. *International Journal of Organization Theory and Behavior*, 9, 510–536.

Beck-Jørgensen, T. (2007). Public values, their nature, stability and change. The case of Denmark. *Public Administration Quarterly*, 30 (4), 365–398.

Beck-Jørgensen, T. & Vrangbæk, K. (2004). *Det offentlige styringsunivers. Fra government til governance?* Århus: Magtutredningen, Århus Universitet.

Beck Jørgensen, T. & Bozeman, B. (2007). Public values. An inventory. *Administration & Society*, 39 (3), 354–381.

Beijaard, D., Meijer, P.C. & Verloop, N. (2004). Reconsidering research on teachers' professional identity. *Teaching and Teacher Education*, 20, 107–128.

Bennington, J. & Moore, M. (2010). Public volume in changing times. In J. Benington & M. Moore (eds), *Public volume theory and practice*. Basingstoke: Palgrave Macmillan.

Blake, R.R. & Mouton J.S. (1964). *The managerial grid*. Houston: Gulf Publishing.

Bligh, M.C., Pearce, C.L & Kohles, J.C. (2006). The importance of self- and shared leadership in team based knowledge work. A meso-level model of leadership dynamics. *Journal of Managerial Psychology*, 21 (4), 296–318.

Bolden, R., Petrov, G. & Gosling, J. (2009). Distributed leadership in higher education. *Educational Management Administration & Leadership*, 37 (2), 257–277.

Bozeman, B. (2007)). *Public values and public interest: Counterbalancing economic individualism*. Washington, DC: Georgetown University Press.

Broadbent, J. & Laughlin, R. (2002). Public service professionals and the New Public Management. In McLaughlin, K., Osborn, S.P. & Ferlie, E. (eds), *New Public Management. Current trends and future prospects*. London: Routledge.

Brookes, S. & Grint, K. (2010). A new public leadership challenge? In Brookes, S. & Grint, K. (eds), *The new public leadership challenge* (1–15). Basingstoke: Palgrave Macmillan.

Brown, M.E. (2002). *Leading with values: The moderating influence of trust on values acceptance by employees*. Unpublished doctoral dissertation, Pennsylvania State University, State College.

Brown, M.E. & Treviño, L.K. (2006). Ethical leadership: A review and future directions. *The Leadership Quarterly*, 17, 595–616.

Brown, P.A., Morris, H.S. & Wilder, W.M. (2006). Ethical exemplification and the AICPA code of professional conduct: An empirical investigation of auditor and public perceptions. *Journal of Business Ethics*, 71, 31–71.

Burns, J. (1978). *Leadership*. New York: Harper and Row.

Burns, T. & Stalker, G.M. (1961). *The management of innovations*. Chicago: Quadrangle Books.

Busch, T. & Wennes, G. (2012). Changing values in the modern public sector: the need for value-based leadership. *The International Journal of Leadership in Public Services*, 8 (4), 201–215.

Busch, T. & Dehlin, E. (2011). *From altruism to egoism – are the images and identity of public sector professionals changing?* Unpublished paper.

Busch, T. & Dehlin, E. (2012). *Utvikling av verdibasert ledelse i kommunal og fylkeskommunal virksomhet*. Rapport Trondheim Økonomiske Høgskole 2012.

Campbell, E. (2008). *Review of the literature. The ethics of teaching as a moral profession*. The Ontario Institute for Studies in Education of the University of Toronto, Curriculum Inquiry 38:4.

Carr, D. (2005). Personal and interpersonal relationship in education and teaching: a virtue ethical perspective. *British Journal of Educational Studies*, 53 (5), 255–271.

Chase, W.G. & Simon, H.A. (1973). Perception in chess. *Cognitive psychology*, 4, 559–572.

Chatman, J. (1991). Matching people and organizations: Selection and socialization in an accounting firm. *Administrative Science Quarterly*, 36, 459–484.

Chi, M.T.H., Glaser, R. & Rees, E. (1982). Expertise in problem solving. In R.J. Sternberg (ed.), *Advances in the psychology of human intelligence*. Hillsdale, NJ: Erlbaum.

Chi, M., Feltowich, P. & Glaser, R. (1981). Categorisation and representation of physics problems by expert and novices. *Cognitive Science*, 5, 121–152.

Christensen, T. & Lægreid, P. (2007). Introduction – theoretical approach and research questions. In Christensen, T. & Lægreid, P. (eds), *Transcending new public management. The transformation of public sector reforms*. Surrey: Ashgate.

Collins, R. (1990). Stratification, emotional energy, and the transient emotions. In T.D. Kemper (ed.), *Research agendas in the sociology of emotions* (27–57). New York: State University of New York.

Colnerud, G. (2006). Teacher ethics as a research problem: syntheses achieved and new issues. *Teacher and Teaching: Theory and Practice*, 12 (3), 365–385.

Conger, J.A. (2000).The vision thing: Exploration into visionary leadership. In Kellerman, B. & Matusak, L. (eds), *Cutting edge: Leadership 2000*. College Park, MD: Center for the advanced study of leadership, University of Maryland.

Conger, J.A. & Kanungo, R. (1998). *Charismatic leadership in organizations.* Thousand Oaks, CA: Sage Publications.

Czarniawska, B. (2000). The European capital of the 2000s. On image construction and modelling. *Corporate Reputation Review,* 3 (3), 202–217.

Day, C. (1999). *Developing teachers. The challenge of lifelong learning.* London: Falmer Press.

Dorfman, P.W., Hanges, P.J. & Brodbeck, F.C. (2004). Leadership and cultural variation: The identification of culturally endorsed leadership profiles. In House, R.J., Hanges, P.J., Javidan, M., Dorfman, P.W. & Gupta, V. (eds), *Culture, leadership, and organizations. The GLOBE study of 62 societies.* London: Sage Publications.

Dreyfus, H.L., Dreyfus, S.E. & Athanasiou, T. (1988). *Mind over machine: The power of human intuition and expertise in the era of the computer.* New York: Free Press.

Driskell, J.E., Copper, C. & Moran, A. (1994). Does mental practice enhance performance? *Journal of Applied Psychology,* 24, 579–591.

Edmondson, A. (1999). Psychological safety and learning behavior in work teams. *Administrative Science Quarterly,* 44 (2), 350–383.

Eide, B.S. (2008). Profesjonsetikkens basis. *Fontene forskning,* 1/08, 38–48.

Eide, T. & Aadland, E. (2008). *Etikkhåndboka for kommunenes helse og omsorgstjenester.* Oslo: Kommuneforlaget.

Fjellvær, H. (2010). *Dual and unitary leadership: Managing ambiguity in pluralistic organizations.* Ph.D. thesis 2010/10, NHH, Bergen, Norway.

Flores, M.A. & Day, C. (2006). Contexts which shape and reshape new teachers' identities: A multi-perspective study. *Teaching and Teacher Education,* 22, 219–232.

Forsyth, D.R. (2006). *Group dynamics.* Belmont, CA: Thompson Wadsworth.

Freidson, E. (2001). *Professionalism. The third logic.* Cambridge: Polity.

Friedrich, T.L., Vessey, W.B., Schuelke, M.J., Ruark, G.A. & Mumford, M.D. (2009). A framework for understanding collective leadership: The selective utilization of leader and team expertise within networks. *The Leadership Quarterly,* 20, 933–958.

Gardner, L.G., Avolio, B.J. & Walumbwa, F.O. (2005). Authentic leadership development: Emergent trends and future directions. In W.L. Gardner, B.J. Avolio & F.O. Walumbwa (eds), *Authentic leadership theory and practice: Origins, effects and development* (387–406). Oxford, UK: Elsevier Science.

Gardner, W.L., Cogliser, C.C., Davis, K.M. & Dickens, M.P. (2011). Authentic leadership: A review of the literature and research agenda. *The Leadership Quarterly,* 22, 1120–1145.

Greenberg, J. (2002). *Managing behavior in organizations.* New Jersey: Pearson Education Inc.

Grint, K. (2010). Wicked problems and clumsy solutions: The role of leadership. In Brookes, S. & Grint, K. (eds), *The new public leadership challenge* (s. 1–15). Basingstoke: Palgrave Macmillan.

Hackman, J.R. (2002). *Leading teams.* Boston: Harvard Business School Press.

Harmon, P. & Evans, K. (1984). When to use cognitive modeling. *Training and Development Journal,* March, 67–68.

Hartley, J. (2010). Political leadership. In Brookes, S. & Grint, K. (eds), *The new public leadership challenge* (s. 133–149). Basingstoke: Palgrave Macmillan.

Hatch, M.J. & Schultz, M. (2002). The dynamics of organizational identity. *Human Relations,* 55, 989–1018.

Hatch, M.J. & Schultz, M. (2008). *Taking brand initiative. How companies can align strategy, culture, and identity through corporate branding.* San Francisco, CA: Jossey-Bass.

Hatton, N. & Smith, D. (1995). Reflection in teacher education: Towards definition and implementation. *Teaching and Teacher Education,* 11 (1), 33–49.

Henderson, S. (2002). Factors impacting on nurses' transference of theoretical knowledge of holistic care into clinical practice. *Nurse Education in Practice,* 2 (4), 244–250.

Hersey, P. & Blanchard, K.H. (1977). *Management of Organizational Behaviour.* Englewood Cliffs, NJ: Prentice Hall.

Hodgkinson, C. (1996). *Administrative philosophy. Values and motivation in administrative life.* Oxford, UK: Pergamon.

Houghton, J.D. & Yoho, S.K. (2005). Toward a contingency model of leadership and psychological empowerment: When should self-leadership be encouraged? *Journal of Leadership & Organizational Studies*, 11, 65–83.

House, R.I. (1996). Path-goal theory of leadership: Lessons, legacy and a reformulated theory. *Leadership Quarterly*, 7, 323–352.

Hunt, G. (2004). The ethics of silence. *Nursing Ethics*, 11, 108–109.

Izard, C.E. (1992). Basic emotions, relations among emotions, and emotion cognition relations. *Psychological Review*, 99, 561–565.

Johnsen, E. (1984). *Introduktion til ledelseslære*. København: Nyt Nordisk Forlag.

Johnsen, E. (2002). *Managing the managerial process: A participative approach*. Copenhagen: DJØF Publ.

Johnsen, E. (2006). *Ledelseslisens*. København: Dafolo Forlag.

Katzenbach, J.R. & Smith, D.K. (1998). *The wisdoms of teams*. London: McGraw Hill.

Kernaghan, K. (2003). Integrating values into public service: The value statement as centerpiece. *Public Administration Review*, 63 (6), 711–719.

Kernis, M.H. (2003). Toward a conceptualization of optimal self-esteem. *Psychological Inquiry*, 14, 1–26.

Klausen, K.K. (1996). *Offentlig organisasjon, strategi og ledelse*. Odense: Odense Universitetsforlag.

Klenke, K. (2005). Corporate values as multi-level, multi-domain antecedents of leader behaviors. *International Journal of Manpower*, 26 (1), 50–66.

Klijn, E-H. (2008). Governance and governance networks in Europe. *Public Management Review*, 10, 505–525.

Kluckhohn, C. (1951). Values and value-orientations in the theory of action: An exploration in definition and classification. In Parsons, T. Shils, E.A. (eds), *Toward a general theory of action* (388–433). Cambridge, MA: Harvard University Press.

Kolb, D.A., Rubin, I.M. & Osland, J.S. (1995). *Organizational behavior: An experimental approach*. Englewood Cliffs, NJ: Prentice Hall.

Kyvik, S. (2009). *The dynamics of change in higher education. Expansion and contraction in an organizational field*. Dordrecht: Springer.

Leach, S., Hartley, J., Lowndes, V., Wilson, D. & Downe, J. (2005). *Local political leadership in the UK*. York: Joseph Rowntree Foundation.

Lewin, K. (1951). *Field theory in social science: Selected theoretical papers*. New York: Norton.

Likert, R. (1979). From production- and employee-centeredness to system 1–4. *Journal of Management*, 5 (2), 147–156.

Locke, E.A. & Latham, G.P. (1990). *A theory of goal setting and task performance*. Englewood Cliffs, NJ: Prentice Hall.

Lundquist, L. (1991). *Etik i offentlig verksamhet*. Lund: Studentlitteratur.

Lundquist, L. (1998). *Demokratins väkare*. Lund: Studentlitteratur.

MacTavish, M.D. & Kolb, J.A. (2008). *An Examination of the Dynamics of Organizational Culture and Values-Based Leader Identities and Behaviors: One Company's Experience*. Paper presented at the Academy of Human Resource Development International Research Conference in the Americas (Panama City, FL, February 20–24, 2008).

Manz, C.C. (1986). Self-leadership: toward an expanded theory of self-influence processes in organizations. *Academy of Management Review*, 11, 585–600.

Manz, C.C & Sims, H.P. jr (1991). Superleadership: Beyond the myth of heroic leadership. *Organizational Dynamics*, 19, 18–35.

Manz, C.C & Sims, H.P. jr (2001). *New superleadership: Leading other to lead themselves*. San Francisco, CA: Berrett-Koehler.

Manz, C.C. & Neck, C.P. (2004). *Mastering self-leadership: Empowering yourself for personal excellence* (Third edition). Upper Saddle River, NJ: Prentice Hall.

Maslow, A. (1954). *Motivation and personality*. New York: Harper and Row.

McAllister, D.J. (1995). Affect and cognition based trust as foundation for interpersonal cooperation in organizations. *Academy of Management Journal*, 38 (1), 24–59.

Meglino, B.M. & Ravlin, E.C. (1998). Individual values in organizations: Concepts, controversies, and research. *Journal of Management*, 24, 351–389.

Melander, P. (1997). Økonomistyring i videnbaserte og politiske organisasjoner – om at implantere økonomisk rationalitet i organisationer, hvor andre værdier er dominerende. *Økonomistyring & Informatikk*, 13, 159–188.

Merton, R.K. (1968). *Social theory and social structure*. New York: The Free Press.

Mintzberg, H. (1983). *Structure in fives: Designing effective organizations*. Englewood Cliffs, NJ: Prentice Hall.

Moore, M.H. (1995). *Creating public value: Strategic management in government*. Cambridge, MA: Harvard University Press.

Mooney, M. (2007). Professional socialization: the key to survival as a newly qualified nurse. *International Journal of Nursing Practice*, 13 (2), 75–80.

Morrell, K. and Hartley J. (2006). A Model of Political Leadership, *Human Relations*, 59, 4, 483–504.

Mowday, R.T., Steers, R.M., & Porter, L.W. (1979): The measurement of organizational commitment. *Journal of Vocational Behavior*, 14, 224–247.

Mullen, B. & Copper, C. (1994). The relation between group cohesiveness and performance: An integration. *Psychological Bulletin*, 115, 2210–2227.

Neck, C.P. & Houghton, J.D. (2006). Two decades of self-leadership theory and research. Past developments, present trends, and futures possibilities. *Journal of Managerial Psychology*, 21, 270–295.

Newell, S., Robertson, M. Scarbrough, H. & Swan, J. (2002). *Managing knowledge work*. Basingstoke: Palgrave Macmillan.

Nonaka, I. & Takeuchi, H. (1995). *The knowledge creating company*. New York: Ford University Press.

Noordegraaf, M. (2007). From "pure" to "hybrid" professionalism. Present-day professionalism in ambiguous public domains, *Administration & Society*, 39 (6), 761–785.

Norwegian Union of Social Educators and Social Workers (2013). http://www.fo.no/getfile. php/01%20Om%20FO/Hefter%20og%20publikasjoner/Yrkesetisk_2011_lav%281%29.pdf (November 18, 2013).

NOU (1991:28) *Mot bedre vitende? Effektiviseringsmuligheter i offentlig sektor*. Norges offentlige utredninger.

Nyeng, F. (2002). *Etikk og økonomi*. Oslo: Abstrakt Forlag.

OECD (2005). *Modernising government. The way forward*. Paris: OECD Publishing.

Olsen, J.P. (1993). Utfordringer for offentlig sektor og for statsvitenskapen. Noen sentrale spørsmål og problemstillinger. *Norsk Statsvitenskapelig Tidsskrift*, 9 (1), 3–28.

Olsen, J.P. (2007). The ups and downs of bureaucratic organization. Working paper no. 14/2007, Arena, Norway.

Ouchi, W.G. (1979). A conceptual framework for the design of organizational control mechanisms. *Management Science*, 25 (9), 833–848.

Øya Community Hospital (2013), http://www.trondheim.kommune.no/content/1117729400/ Oya-helsehus---Information-in-english (November 18, 2013).

Öztürk, S. (2010). The opinions of preschool teachers about ethical principles. *Educational Sciences: Theory and Practice*, 10 (1), 393–418.

Pearce, C.L. & Conger, J.A. (2003). All those years ago: The historical underpinnings of shared leadership. In C.L. Pearce & J.A. Conger (eds), *Shared leadership. Reframing the hows and whys of leadership* (1–18). Thousand Oaks, CA: Sage Publications.

Pearce, C.L. (2004). The future of leadership: Combining vertical and shared leadership to transform knowledge work. *Academy of Management Executive*, 18, 47–57.

Polanyi, M. (1974). *Personal knowledge: Towards a post-critical philosophy*. Chicago: University of Chicago Press.

Pollach, I. (2005). Corporate self-presentation on the www. Strategies for enhancing usability, credibility and utility. *Corporate Communications: An International Journal*, 10 (4), 285–301.

Pollitt, C. (2003). *The essential public manager*. Maidenhead, Philadelphia: Open University Press.

Pollitt, C. & Bouckaert, G. (2011). Public management reform: A comparative analysis – New public management, governance and the neo-weberian state. Oxford: Oxford University Press.

Porter, C.W. & Lawler, E.E. (1968). *Managerial attitudes and performance*. Homewood, IL: Irwin.

Porter, L.W. & McLaughlin, G.B. (2006). Leadership and the organizational context: Like the weather? *Leadership Quarterly*, 17, 559–576.

Quinn, R.E. (1988). *Beyond rational management: Mastering the paradoxes and competing demands of high performance*. San Francisco: Jossey-Bass.

Rassin, M. (2008). Nurses' professional and personal values. *Nursing Ethics*, 15 (5), 614–630.

Ravasi, D. & van Rekom, J. (2003). Key issues in organizational identity and identification theory. *Corpoarate Reputation Review*, 6 (2), 118–132.

Riketta, M. (2005). Organizational identification: A meta-analysis. *Journal of Vocational Behavior*, 66, 358–384.

Rokeach, M. (1973). *The nature of human values*. New York: Free Press.

Rokeach, M. (1976). The nature of human values and value systems. In Hollander, E.P. & Hunt, R.G. (eds), *Current perspectives in social psychology*. New York: Oxford University Press.

Røvik, K.A. (2007). *Trender og translasjoner. Ideer som former det 21. århundrets organisasjon*. Oslo: Universitetsforlaget.

Rutgers, M.R. (2008). Sorting out public values? On the contingency of value classification in public administration. *Administrative Theory & Praxis*, 30 (1), 92–113.

Ryan, R.M. & Deci, E.L. (2003). On assimilating identities to the self: A self-determination theory perspective on internalization and integrity within cultures. In M.R. Leary & J.P. Tangney (eds), *Handbook of self and identity* (253–272). New York: Free Press.

Sand, I-J. (2004). Stat og ledelse i det polycentriske samfunn. In Pedersen, D. (ed.), *Offentlig ledelse i managementstaten*. København, Samfunnslitteratur.

Schein, E. (1978). *Career dynamics: Matching individual and organizational needs*. Reading, MA: Addison-Wesley.

Schein, E. (1988). *Organizational psychology* (3rd edition). Englewood Cliffs, NJ: Prentice Hall.

Schein, E. (2010). *Organizational culture and leadership* (4. utg.). San Francisco, CA: Jossey Bass.

Schultz, M. (1995). On studying organizational culture – diagnosis and understanding. Berlin: Walter de Gruyter.

Scott, W.R. (1995). *Institutions and organizations*. Thousand Oaks: Sage.

Selznick, P. (1957). *Leadership in administration*. New York: Harper & Row.

Shamir, B., House, R.J. & Arthur, M.B. (1993). The motivational effects of charismatic leadership: A self-concept based theory. *Organizational Science*, 6, 19–47.

Shaw, H.K. & Degazon, C. (2008). Integrating the core professional values of nursing: A profession, not just a career. *Journal of Cultural Diversity*, 15 (1), 44–50.

Sjøvold, E. (2010). *Teamet. Utvikling, effektivitet og endring i grupper*. Oslo: Universitetsforlaget.

Søholm, T.M. & Juhl, A. (2005). Udvikling av det højtydende team. In Storch, J. & Søholm, T.M. (eds), *Teambaserte organisasjoner i praksis*. København: Dansk Psykologisk Forlag.

Sørensen, E. (2007). Public administration as megagovernance. In Gjeldsstrup, G. & Sørensen, E. (eds), *Public administration in transition*. København: DJØF Publishing.

Stevens, C.U., D'Intino, R.S. & Victor, B. (1995). The moral quandary of transformational leadership: Change for whom? *Research in Organizational Change and Development*, 8, 123–143.

Swartz, S.H. (1992). Universals in the content and structure of values: Theory and empirical tests in 20 countries. In Zanna, M. (ed.), *Advances in experimental social psychology* (vol. 25, 1–65). New York, Academic Press.

Tampoe, M. (1993). Motivating knowledge workers: The challenge for the 1990's. *Long Range Planning*, 26 (3), 49–55.

Tannenbaum, R. & Schmidt, W.H. (1958). How to choose a leadership pattern. *Harvard Business Review*, 36 (2), 95–101.

Thompson, G.F. (2001). *Between hierarchies and markets. The logics and limits of network forms of organization*. Oxford and New York: Oxford University Press.

Thyssen, O. (2009). *Business ethics and organizational values: A systems-theoretical analysis*. Basingstoke: Palgrave Macmillan.

Treviño, L.K., Hartman, L.P. & Brown, M. (2000). Moral person and moral manager: How executives develop a reputation for ethical leadership. *California Management Review*, 42, 128–142.

Uhl-Bien, M. (2006). Relational leadership theory: Exploring the social processes of leadership and organizing. *The Leadership Quarterly*, 17, 654–676.

Veenman, S. (1984). Perceived problems of beginning teachers. *Review of Educational Research*, 54 (2), 143–178.

Vroom, V. (1964). *Work and motivation*. New York: Wiley.

Vroom, V.H. & Yetton, P.W. (1973). *Leadership and decision-making*. Pittsburg: University of Pittsburg Press.

Wæraas, A. (2010). Communicating identity: A study of core value statements in regulative institutions. *Administration & Society*, 42, 5, 526–549.

Walumbwa, F.O., Wang, P., Wang, H., Schaubroeck, J. & Avolio, B.J. (2010). Psychological processes linking authentic leadership to follower behaviors. *The Leadership Quarterly*, 21, 901–914.

Weber, M. (1978). *Economy and society: An outline of interpretive sociology*. Redigert av G. Roth & C. Wittich. Berkley, CA: University of California Press.

Wenger, E. (1998). *Communities of practice. Learning, meaning and identity*. Cambridge: Cambridge University Press.

Wilensky, H.L. (1964). The Professionalization of Everyone? *The American Journal of Sociology*, 70, 2, 137–158.

Yukl, G. (2006). *Leadership in organizations*. Upper Saddle River, NJ: Pearson Prentice Hall.

Index